THE GREAT
COVER-UP

A CONDOM COMPENDIUM

THE GREAT
COVER-UP

A CONDOM COMPENDIUM

Written by
Susan Zimet and Victor Goodman

Illustrated by
Stephanie Silber

CIVAN, INC. New York

Published by Civan, Inc., New York
Copyright © 1988 by Civan, Inc.
All Rights Reserved
Cover and Text Design by Nava Atlas

Library of Congress Cataloging in Publication Data

Zimet, Susan and Goodman, Victor
The Great Cover-up
Condoms. I. Title
ISBN 0-9621700-0-3
Library of Congress Catalog Number 88-92769

Printed in the United States of America
First Printing

Dedicated to our parents for not using
a condom when we were conceived.

And to Andrew Eli for always putting life
in its proper perspective.

ACKNOWLEDGMENTS

When working on any long project there is always a plethora of people who help with advice, expertise and moral support. Authors are lucky in that they have an opportunity to put their thanks in print.

First of all, our never ending thanks to Stephanie Silber for her illustrations, writing, editing, and most importantly, her incredible support and enthusiasm for this project.

Many thanks also go to Nava Atlas for her cover design, layout advice, and patience in helping two neophytes through the process of printing a book.

Many thanks and much respect to Scott Hoyt and everyone at Carter-Wallace for opening their library to us as well as their help throughout this project.

For being constant creative sounding-boards for words and ideas, our thanks go to Lynda Auerbach, Vicky Cooper, Robert Zimet, and Victor Zimet.

To Roslyn and Jack Zimet, Ruth and Lou Barbanell, and Arlyne and Ed McMullin, our love and most sincere thanks for their eternal support.

For their enthusiasm and advice in getting this project started, our thanks to Ashley and Russel Leiman and Eugene Beer of Banyan Books.

We owe many thanks to all the following friends and relatives for their help or moral support, late-night phone calls with condom jokes and critiques, and for listening to us talk about condoms for the last year: Victor Barbanell; Amy Berkower and Alan Zuckerman of Writer's House; Sheri Berenbaum; Joann Crovets; Mike Cunio; Linda Davidson; Dave Edwards; Carol Einbeinder; Dan Fischer of Classic Colour; Dan Glickman; Sherry Harris; Kenneth Hirsh; Sue, Ed, Joe, Annie, Rikki Horwitz; Bruce Hosmer; Ellen Jacobs; Marty Klar, Lorraine Lecesne; Seymour and Jan Miles; Barry V. Miller; Terri Savago; Marc and Karen Shapiro Wolens; Steve and Donna Schwartz of RiverRun Press; Pat Connelly Smith; Chaim Tabak; Carol and John Waldman; Dan Weiss; Richard and Wendy Zackon; George Zeigler.

These acknowledgments would be incomplete without mentioning the New York City Public Library, the Sojourner Truth Library at SUNY–New Paltz, and the Elting Memorial Library in New Paltz. Also for photocopying above and beyond the call of duty, thanks to everyone at P.D.Q. Copy Shop in New Paltz and Larchmont Copy Shop.

And last, though certainly not least, we must thank Steve Auerbach for his willingness to share his home and life, for putting up with late hours and temperaments, and for all the countless ways in which he contributed to the making of this book.

A compilation such as this could never have been feasible without the permission of so many. A lot of time and effort was spent trying to clear copyrights for all the quotes, excerpts and illustrations used in this book. Our apologies to anyone we overlooked and our grateful acknowledgments to the following:

P. 27 — From 1987, Katie Leishman, as originally published in the February 1987 issue of Atlantic Monthly: Russ Reade quote

P. 37 — From Cosmopolitan: quote by Lee Ann

P. 74 — Ibid: quote by Russell Friedman

P. 83 — Ibid: Helen Gurley Brown quote

P. 9 — ©Discover 1987, Family Media, Inc.: Dudley Castle and 18th century aristocratic family excerpts

P.112 — From July 1983, Bob Greene article in Esquire, Sterling Lord Realistic, agent: Wilbur Halloway and Cindy Gerner quote

P.109 — Fortune Magazine, Nov. 24, 1986: son-in-law of Walter H. Annenberg excerpt

P. 32 — From Sept. 1987, Sara Nelson, Glamour Magazine. Courtesy author and Glamour. Copyright © 1987 by The Condé Nast Publications, Inc.: quote by Frank

P. 33 — Ibid: quote by Martha

P. 36 — From Oct. 1986, Dave Barry, Glamour Magazine. Courtesy author, Fox Chase Agency, Glamour. Copyright © 1986 by The Condé Nast Publications, Inc.: quote by author

P.101 — From March 1987, Glamour: quote about Don Johnson. Courtesy Glamour. Copyright © 1987 by The Condé Nast Publications, Inc.

P. 30 — From Aug. 1984, David Weinberg, Mademoiselle. Courtesy of author and Mademoiselle. Copyright © 1984 by The Condé Nast Publications, Inc.

P. 30 — From spring 1985, Stephen Williams, courtesy of Men's Health: Japanese businessman quote.

P. 94 — Ibid: quote by Mr. Okamoto and Fuji Latex beauty contest excerpt.

P. 52 — From Aug. 15, 1988, Newsweek. Courtesy of Frank Pogue and Newsweek: quote by Frank Pogue

P.112 — From Feb. 16, 1987, Newsweek. Courtesy of Newsweek: gas station restroom operator quote.

P. 30 — From July 23, 1987, Amy Pagnozzi and Mel Jaffe, New York Post: quote by authors.

P. 33 — Ibid: quotes by Jackie D'Amico and 31-year-old research analyst.

P. 43 — From Sept. 15, 1987, Ray Kerrison, New York Post: quote by author. Reprinted by permission of New York Post. Copyright © 1987 New York Post Co., Inc.

P. 25 — From April 5, 1987, Francis X. Clines, New York Times: Monique quote.

P. 26 — From March 19, 1987, Philip M. Boffey, New York Times: Jerry De Jong excerpt.

P. 33 — From June 3, 1987, James Barron, New York Times: quote from Letty Cottin Pogrebin.

P. 39 — From June 1, 1988, Katherine Bishop, New York Times: Hene Kelly excerpt.

P. 49 — From Oct. 11, 1987 New York Times: Dr. Loring Hart quote.

P. 77 — From Sept. 27, 1987, Erik Eckholm, New York Times: Dr. James Chin quote.

P. 96 — From April 6, 1987 New York Times: quote from Mrs. Koop. Copyright © 1987/88 by the New York Times Company. Reprinted by permission.

P. 35 — From March 14, 1988, People. Courtesy of People: quotes by Brooks Brothers saleswoman and New York writer.

P. 19 — From Jan. 21, 1987, Neill Borowski, Philadelphia Inquirer: quote by Judith Cohen. Courtesy of Philadelphia Inquirer.

P. 85 — From June 1987, Robert Coram, Playboy: quote by author.

P. 86 — Ibid: quote by anonymous A.I.D. worker and other A.I.D. excerpts. Originally appeared in Playboy Magazine: Permission granted by author.

P.101 — From June 1987, Playboy: quote by Linda Ellerbee.

P.107 — From Sept. 1987, Playboy: bowling alley excerpt.

P. 38 — From July 1987, David Seeley, Playboy: quote by Chris. Originally appeared in Playboy Magazine: Permission granted by author. Copyright © 1987 by Playboy.

P.101 — From Dec. 29, 1986, Rubber and Plastic News: quote by ABC spokesperson.

P. 78 — From Jan. 1987, Carolyn Jabs, Self. Courtesy of author, John Graves, and Self. Copyright © 1986 by The Condé Nast Publications, Inc.: quote by John Graves.

P. 78 — From Feb. 16, 1987, Time. Permission granted by Dr. Maisonet: quote by Dr. Maisonet.

P. 33 — From June 2, 1986, U.S. News & World Report. Permission granted by Shirley Zussman: quote by Shirley Zussman.

P. 41 — From March 30, 1987, U.S. News & World Report: quote by Secretary of Education.

P.101 — From Feb. 23, 1987, U.S. News & World Report: quote by Rep. Henry Waxman. Courtesy of U.S. News & World Report © 1987.

P. 77 — From Jan. 1987, Washingtonian. Courtesy of Washingtonian: quote by Dr. Cecil Fox.

P. 31 — From Oct. 1985, Working Woman: quote by female condom customer.

Our grateful acknowledgments to: Art Buchwald, Lucille Davis, London International Group, Virgin Records, Jiffi North America, Ansell Inc., Schmid Laboratories, Inc., The Pet Rubber Company, Karen Hughes of The National Condom Week Resource Center and Carter Wallace Inc. for all their help in making this project a reality.

Grateful acknowledgment to the following for their kind permission to reproduce the following illustrations:

P.   4 — Charles O. Hoyt

P.   5 — The Library of Congress

P.   7 — The Wellcome Institute Library, London

P.   9 — Trustees of the British Museum, London

P. 12 — The Library of Congress

P. 19 — National Archives Trust Fund Board

P. 22 — National Archives Trust Fund Board

P. 48 — Bense Design Concept (Valerie Randell-Art Direction and Design, Chris Hansen-Illustrator)

P. 53 — Shelly Horowitz

P. 89 — Battelle Seattle Research Center San Francisco Press, Inc.

Special thanks to Shelly Horowitz for her artwork and advice; Bill Lee of Penthouse; Marcia Terrones of Playboy; Barbara Snow of Planned Parenthood Federation, Inc.

CONTENTS

PLEASE NOTE: The words in bold face within the text are synonyms for condoms. For a complete list, see Appendix One.

INTRODUCTION

This book is not an AIDS book, nor is it meant to promote promiscuity. It does try, however, to face the reality that this country is in the midst of an alarming rise not only in AIDS but in all sexually transmitted diseases (STDs). Also, the United States has the highest number of unwanted pregnancies in the western world.

Condoms are the one device that can help reduce these social problems. They are the only means we have that help reduce the risk of STDs and at the same time are a safe and effective means of birth control. But bear in mind—short of abstinence and no-risk sex practices such as kissing, hugging, and masturbation, nothing is one hundred percent safe against STDs and unwanted births.

However, a properly used condom will reduce the risk of STDs and unplanned pregnancies. If you have any questions on any form of birth control, please consult your physician.

SOME FOOD FOR THOUGHT:

- Every thirty seconds a U.S. teenager becomes pregnant. (That's over 1 million per year or 1 in 6 of all pregnancies.)

- 77% of teen pregnancies are unintentional. Of the mothers only ½ will graduate high school. Only ½ will marry the father of the child, and only ⅓ of these marriages will survive.

- Every two and a half seconds an American contracts an STD. (That is approximately 12 million per year.)

- One in four Americans aged 13–50 will acquire at least 1 STD in their lifetime.

- This year 1 million Americans will be infected with gonorrhea, 1 million with genital warts, 3 million with trichomoniasis, 2½ million with urethritis and chlamydia, 70 thousand with syphilis, close to ½ million with genital herpes.

- This year 100,000 women will become sterile because of STDs.

- By 1991 it is predicted that AIDS will be the leading cause of death among 25- to 44-year-olds. (Costing Americans 12–17 billion dollars per year.)

- 609 teenagers a day contract gonorrhea or syphilis.

Since condoms will be a fact of life in the foreseeable future, we need to learn how to integrate them into our daily life the way we do any personal care product. Chapter Six in this book will teach you how to talk about condoms without embarrassment. You'll also learn how to incorporate condoms into your lovemaking so they may actually enhance the experience. Finally, this book will serve as a conversation starter for what can often be a hard subject to bring up.

CHAPTER ONE

HISTORY

GRANDMA'S CONDOM RECIPE

In the 1800s condom recipes were found in many home remedy books:

- Take the intestines of a sheep and soak in water
- Turn inside out and then soak in a weak alkaline solution
- Scrape and then disinfect with vapor from burning brimstone
- Wash, blow up, and dry
- Cut to proper length and tie with ribbon at end

THE NAME GAME

The origin of the word condom has caused much debate.

The best known legend is that of Dr. Condom, a physician in the court of King Charles II (1660–1685) who was knighted for his invention of a **sheath** used to stop the spread of both disease and the king's bastards (of whom he acknowledged fourteen.)

Richter, a German etymologist, believed it can be traced back to the Persian 'kondu,' which was a storage vessel made from animal intestines.

Another etymologist, Hans Ferdy, claimed the word derived from the Latin verb 'condere,' which means to conceal, protect, or preserve.

And for those who have been there . . .

Some believe the word comes from this small town in Gascony, France, which has a reputation for high living.

THE GREAT COVER-UP

Men might be better off if their reproductive organs were on the inside of their body. However, since they are not, men have been covering their privates (or colonels, depending on how they are built) for years.

These coverings have been used as:

- Mini shields during combat
- Good luck pieces to promote fertility
- Status symbols (different colors for different ranks)
- Protection against tropical disease and insect bites
- Cover-ups for modesty's sake
- Amulets to ward off evil spirits

And if you're ever in New Guinea, don't be surprised when you see the men tapping their **sheaths** in heated conversation—they are only trying to make a point.

A sketch from a XIX Dynasty (1350–1200 BC) original depicts an ancient Egyptian wearing a sheath for decoration.

OKRA VS. SILK

Man has been ingenious not only in the uses of a **sheath** but the material they're made of:

- Rumor has it—Roman soldiers made sheaths from the muscles of dead foes.

- The Djuka Indians had a five-inch okra-type pod, closed at one end, that was inserted into the woman for the man to come into.

- Japanese Kabutogata (hard helmets) and Kowagata (penis sacks) were made of tortoiseshell, horns and leather. Speculation has it they were used as dildos by women and to help impotent men.

- The Chinese made coverings out of oiled silk paper, Europeans used fish bladder, and Egyptians used papyrus soaked in water.

SEASONAL SEX

Not everyone in Japan was happy during the summer before the advent of rubber condoms. For birth control, sun-dried membranes of the Kuichi Kugai, a bamboo-shaped crustacean, were used. Unfortunately, these "condoms" had a short storage life and the crustaceans just weren't around in the summer.

GLAD BAGS

"The **overcoat** that puts one's mind at rest."

—Memoires de Casanova,
1863

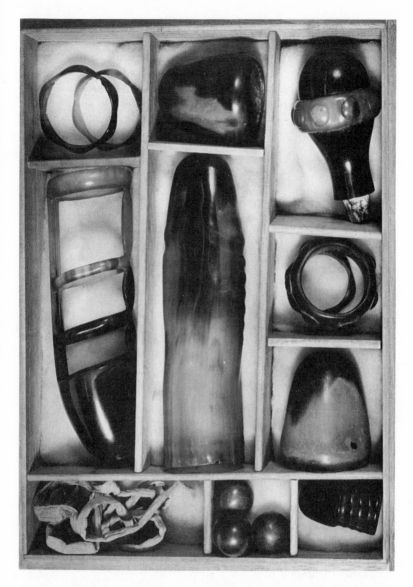

Japanese 'Happy Box' showing toys of sexual amusement. It contains various tortoise shell **sheaths** *and bells which are slipped into the vagina for musical accompaniment.*

SCORPION SEMEN

The first written mention of a **sheath** is found in the saga of Minos, King of Crete. It seems old Minos had a slight problem of serpents and scorpions in his semen. The remedy—a goat bladder slipped inside the woman to catch the snake load.

Once free of these demons, he was able to copulate without worry with his beloved wife.

KAMA SUTRA

The Kama Sutra of Vastyayano (300 AD) shows that India knew of penis coverings as early as 300 AD. However, the ones described may not have been in everyday use, since they were designed to provide pleasure to an "elephant woman."

Materials recommended included silver, gold, copper, iron, buffalo horn, lead, wood, tin, or ivory with rings of different dimensions included to heighten arousal.

MORE GLAD BAGS

"The little preventive **bags** by the English to save the fair sex from anxiety . . ."

—*Memoires de Casanova,*
1863

GABRIELLO FALLOPIUS (1523–1562)

Gabriello Fallopius was a doctor who concentrated on things below the waist. He is most famous for his discovery of the fallopian tubes.

A lesser known fact: Gabriello invented a medicated linen **sheath**—the first to be used for protection against venereal disease. He reported on tests of 1,100 men that showed not one developed a venereal disease.

What happened to the women is not mentioned. Dr. Fallopius also dispensed advice to parents to "take every pain in infancy to enlarge the privy members [of boys] since a well grown specimen never comes amiss!"

LESSON IN LOVE

In the book *L'Escole des Filles* (School for Girls, 1655), students were taught that a condom was "a little piece of linen" on the tip of the penis, placed so that it could "receive the lacquer of love."

OLD *BAGS*

In the latrines of Dudley Castle in Warwickshire, England, archaeologists found the remains of five rather crumbled condoms among the remnants of a feast of boar, venison and lamb. Dating back to 1646, they are believed to be the oldest in the world.

When an early nineteenth-century aristocratic family donated some papers to the British Museum, an added prize were the eighteenth-century condoms found among the pages. At that time they were kept hidden from public view because they were deemed too erotic.

Today they are still not on open display because of potential damage from light.

An 18th-century condom found in the British Museum. Condom was tied at the end with a red ribbon.

BEATING AROUND THE BUSH

Mme. de Sévigné (1671) describes a sheath of goldbeaters skin she claimed was an "armour against pleasure, gossamer against infection."

Goldbeaters skin, for those of you who weren't around in the seventeenth century, was used as a covering for bottles of precious fluids and was made from the same part of the lamb used to make condoms.

EQUAL OPPORTUNITY

Joseph Gay's *The Petticoat: An Heroi* (1716), was one of the few references to condoms that recommended them for honorable women, not just prostitutes.

So might the Fair, thus arm'd remain secure
And brave the dangers which they shun'd before.

WILL THE REAL MRS. PHILLIPS PLEASE STAND UP?

To guard your self from shame or fear
Votaries to Venus, hasten here;
None in our wares e'er found a flaw,
Self preservation's nature's law.

This poem ended a handbill that advertised *Mrs. Phillips's bladder policies* or *implements of safety*. The confusing part is that there was more than one Mrs. Phillips using this poem.

It seems the original Mrs. Phillips sold her condom business to a Mrs. Mary Perkins but some 10 years later decided to re-enter the business. What ensued was a handbill war with each claiming the other was dead and that they had the original and superior quality goods.

THE FRENCH LETTER

A French description (1714) of a condom: "an enchanted **armour**" to be put over the "instrument of pleasure" at the moment the "gallant" was ready to thrust forward.

ERECTOR HIMSELF

White Kennett, son of the Bishop of Peterborough and a rector himself, praised condoms in a poem entitled "The **Machine**" (1724) that was subsequently changed to "Love's Preservation."

Hear and attend: In condom's praise
I sing and thou, O Venus! Aid my lays
By machine secure, the willing maid
Can taste love's joys, nor is she more afraid
Her swelling belly should, or squalling brat,
Betray the luscious pastime she has been at!

JAMES BOSWELL—1740–1795

"At the bottom of the Haymarket I picked up a strong, jolly young damsel, and taking her under the arm I conducted her to Westminster Bridge, and then in **armour** complete did I engage her upon this noble edifice. The whim of doing it there with the Thames rolling below us amused me much."

"The house at Covent Garden was much crowded; so I left my place to Nairne, went and drank tea with Mrs. Brown, then came to the park, and in **armorial guise** performed concubinage with a strong, plump, good-humoured girl called Nanny Baker."

—April 1763
Boswell's London Journal
(1762–63)

CASANOVA (1725–1798)

"The girl came back with the packet of twelve condoms. I put myself in the right position, and ordered her to choose one that fitted well. Sulkily, she began examining and measuring. 'This one doesn't fit well,' I told her. 'Try another.' Another, and another; and suddenly I splashed her well and truly."

—Histoire de ma Vie

Casanova was one of the few men of his time to use condoms not only as a barrier against disease but also as a means of birth control. He was also known to blow them up to amuse the ladies.

EVERYONE MUST FIND HIS OWN SOLUTION

That famous man about town and many other places, the Marquis de Sade, talks of three birth control methods in his *La Philosophie dans le Boudoir,* written in 1795. First was the condom, next the sponge, and lastly, his personal favorite, anal coitus, which he found "la plus delicieuse sans doute."

BALLOONS ARE RISING

At the Theatre Royal in Covent Garden in 1823, Mr. Rayner sang the following verse about condoms.

SUNG TO THE TUNE OF "BOW WOW WOW"

Balloons are all improving fast,
and with each other vie, Sirs,
In public estimation they seem
Rising very high, Sirs,
For swiftness in their journeys,
They were never known to fail, Sir,
They always travel past and never
Go without a male, Sirs.

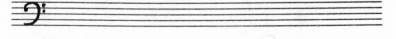

PENNY LANE

The Beatles exhibited their knowledge of condom history when they wrote "Penny Lane." Back in the 1800s Penny Lane was a street infamous for its night life.

The barbers they mention refer to the uniquely British practice of barbershops (until recently) being the major retail outlet for condoms.

The portrait of the Queen in the man's pocket is a reference to condoms that were made in the late 1800s bearing pictures of Queen Victoria (others had Prime Minister Gladstone). The fire engine mentioned is kept clean by a "**machine,**" which was a euphemism for condoms.

AH, IT WAS A VERY GOOD YEAR

The era of rubberized condoms began in 1843 when Goodyear and Hancock vulcanized rubber.

To promote rubber items, Goodyear published thick catalogs. Ironically, he included vulcanized vaginal pessaries but omitted the condom.

Despite that omission, by the turn of the century, rubber condoms became one of the most popular forms of birth control.

REDESIGNING THE RUBBER *RAINCOAT*

1843–1849	Up to 1901	1901	1930's

  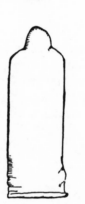 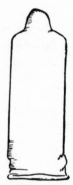

Short condoms just cover the tip

Full-length condoms with a seam

Seam gone. Teat-end introduced

Condoms no longer have to be laundered with the invention of the latex process

IMPROVING THE *CONEY ISLAND WHITEFISH*

Slow down, you come too fast, you've got to make the moment last . . . now there is a condom with a local anesthetic.

For that great cover-up, a condom has been designed that even covers the scrotum.

In the heat of the moment, do you have trouble finding enough hands to put on a condom? The Kenbi Company of Japan has developed one that can be put on single-handedly.

For the future . . . packages that glow in the dark . . . biodegradable condoms . . . sized condoms—just think of all the fun in the fitting!

> "Women buy brassieres in A, B, and C cups, and pantyhose in different sizes, and I think it would help condom efficacy, that we should package them in different sizes and maybe label them like olives: jumbo, colossal and supercolossal so that men didn't have to go in and ask for small."
>
> —Barbara Seaman
> (American writer
> testifying before U.S.
> Senate Committee)

The Japanese just came out with musical condoms. That's right, musical condoms. Similar to musical greeting cards, they work off a microchip at the base of the condom. The song, appropriately enough, is "Love Me Do" by the Beatles.

THE TIMES, THEY ARE A-CHANGING

Are condoms a prophylactic against disease or a form of contraception? If you answered "both," you would not have been legally correct until 1977.

For over 100 years, laws such as the National Comstock Law (1873) made it illegal to disseminate any information related to birth control, let alone sell condoms as a contraceptive. It wasn't until 1965 that the Supreme Court upheld a *married* couple's right to practice birth control.

In 1977, the Supreme Court finished doing legally what the sexual revolution had already done morally by declaring unconstitutional all state laws that prohibited the dissemination of information, distribution and display of condoms as a contraceptive.

TODAY'S SITUATION

"Formerly, under hypocritical laws, condoms were labeled 'For Prevention of Disease Only.' Then the U.S. Supreme Court struck down the hypocritical laws and we began to stress condoms as contraceptives, both in labeling and advertising. Now, with the AIDS epidemic, we're back to stressing the prophylactic features."

—Mark Klein,
marketing manager

OUT WITH THE OLD; IN WITH THE NEW

What do you do with 365 used rubbers? Make them into a tire and call it a Goodyear.

CHAPTER TWO

WAR STORIES

SAFETY MEASURES

In the early 1900s the U.S. Navy distributed condoms to sailors before shore leave to protect them from V.D. The powers that be looked to end this practice; however, WWI brought with it a rapid spread of venereal disease.

In the first 17 months of the war 280,000 soldiers contracted V.D. This forced the army to spend one million dollars on condoms and sex education.

"IF YOU CAN'T SAY NO TAKE A PRO"

The above slogan spearheaded a U.S. Army educational campaign to get the men into the "proper" uniform for late night maneuvers. The Army created stations to sell a package of three condoms with lubricant for ten cents (in some places free). However, when women manned the counters, sales fell off, so vending machines were substituted. By the end of the war these centers were selling or giving away fifty million condoms per month.

BEGINNING OF THE END

Some believe the event that truly marks the end of the Victorian era was when the British government issued condoms to the troops in 1917.

WAR LESSONS

Soldiers came back from WWI with its lesson on condoms well learned—prior to WWI, Baltimoreans purchased 2.5 million condoms a year. After the war, sales rose to 6.3 million.

MILITARY STRATEGY

During WWII, the military, in its battle against sexually transmitted diseases used the "score technique," which was a policy that emphasized the use of condoms. In the 1950s, with the advent of penicillin, the battle plan changed to one of "character guidance." To keep those young eyes (and other parts) from roving, companies were ordered to spend at least one hour a week "building character."

DANGLE PARADES

During WWI, New Zealand was much admired for how they faced the problem of V.D. among the troops. Naturally, there was a wide distribution of chemical prophylaxis and condoms. But "Dangle Parades," held to ensure early diagnosis and treatment of disease, were the cornerstone of their effort.

THE CUTTING EDGE

In an effort to save rubber for the war effort, nylon condoms were tested. These condoms provided too much static electricity, too little sensation, and could become so hard they could develop a cutting edge. Ouch!

World War II Poster

DOUBLE STANDARDS

In order to insure the future supply of soldiers to carry on the Aryan race, condoms were banned to the general public by Himmler as WWII approached. But the crack troops of the Wehrmacht were ordered to use them so they would not be pulled out of the fight because of venereal disease.

CLOSE TO THE SOURCE

In 1940 the Japanese set up a condom factory in Peking so their military would have a source of needed supplies close at hand.

ANY BASEBALL CARDS TO TRADE?

Along with cigarettes, condoms became a highly prized and barterable possession in the British army during WWII.

CONSCRIPTED CONDOMS

Afraid of getting caught in the trenches with your pants down? You need not worry if you're in the Swedish army. Introducing "Commando," camouflaged condoms that will be given to the 45,000 conscripted soldiers.

COVER YOUR BUTT—RIFLE BUTT, THAT IS

The military realized the versatility of condoms when during the amphibious landing at Dunkirk in 1942, they issued them to the Allied troops to cover their rifle barrels.

MILITARY SOLUTIONS

In a misguided attempt to stop the spread of syphilis, the Navy actually removed the door handles on battleship hatchways to cut down on casual contact.

One of the Army solutions in its war against V.D. was to close down 110 red light districts around the U.S. and to incarcerate 20,000 to 30,000 prostitutes.

Eventually, to enforce "moral behavior," the military leaders made it a court-martial offense to contract syphilis.

HE FORGOT HIS RUBBERS

Allegro Moderato

Words & Music by Bobby Gregory & Joe Davis

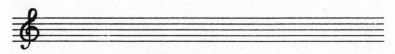

Verse: Wear your **rubbers**, nev-er get your feet wet—that's what the doctor said to Johnny Wat-er; But he has-n't learned to be discreet yet, he ig-nores his doc-tor's or-ders;

Chorus: One night John-ny took a walk, And he for-got his rub-bers; With his girl he stopped to talk, and soon he missed his rub-bers;

Verse: For just when they were in a huddle The rain came down and what a puddle; He was rea-lly "on the spot" for he forgot his rub-bers rub-bers.

Verse: For they had hardly got to-gether When sud-den-ly came storm-y weath-er The rain came down 'twas quite dis-pleas-ing

Verse: For she walked off and left him sneez-ing He was real-ly "on the spot" for he for-got his rub-bers rub-bers.

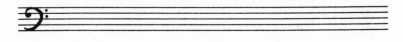

CHAPTER THREE

A VIEW FROM THE STREET

HIGH PRICED SEX

"But crazy hookers—the addicts up by the canal bridge—are selling sex without condoms for higher prices and there are customers who think that's exotic. Can you believe?"

—Monique, 23 years old
Dutch prostitute

HOUSE OF THE RISING SUN

"It was the toughest business decision I ever made. Now prostitutes are calling up from all over looking for a job."

—Russ Reade, owner of the Chicken Ranch (a legal house of prostitution in Nevada), commenting on his decision to institute a house rule that customers must always use condoms for all sex acts.

LADIES OF THE NIGHT: UNITE

Believe it or not, the Australian Prostitute Collective has become state funded and now distributes free condoms and safe sex advice to customers in Kings Cross, Sydney's red light district.

GETTING TO THE BOTTOM OF A SMALL PROBLEM

Australian men have complained that condoms from Japan and Taiwan are too small for them. The New South Wales Parliamentary Committee on Prostitution has hired an investigator to check this out. We wonder if it's a private dick.

EDUCATIONAL PORN SHOPS

Massage parlors and adult bookstores in West Hollywood, California must supply their customers with information on AIDS and safe sex if they want their licenses renewed.

BETTER TO GIVE THAN TO RECEIVE

"One of his [Jerry De Jong, a 30-year-old drug abuse counselor in San Francisco] most difficult clients was a transsexual prostitute and drug addict who was infected with the AIDS virus and presumably spreading it to her customers and fellow addicts.

"At first she insisted that her customers would never accept condoms. So, one day in August, Mr. De Jong took sexual paraphernalia to her room and spent an hour and a half demonstrating how easily a condom could be applied. He blew up 25 condoms like balloons, giving the room a festive appearance as prostitutes and addicts gathered to hear his talk on avoiding AIDS."

—*New York Times,*
March 1987

Hey, it's safe to share my needle, I'm wearing a condom!

RATED X (FOR THOSE OVER 18)

Porn magazines of the '80s now intersperse six-letter words like "condom" among the four-letter ones:

"Before I got too excited she pulled out another rubber and pulled it onto my engorged tool . . . I guess she was afraid of catching a disease."

—From a porn magazine
of the '80s

PRISONER OF SEX

It is illegal for prisoners to have sex with other inmates. But let's face it—what can you do with these guys if they break that law—put them in jail?!

So, in April 1987, the State of Vermont began giving condoms away to those prisoners who requested them.

New York City, being a little bit more reserved, decided in 1987 to test condoms by giving them away to 90 homosexual inmates in Rikers Island Prison. Although the criteria are not known, if the test proves successful, the program will be expanded throughout the state prison system.

However, the Reagan administration was having none of it. They know that homosexual acts are a violation of prison regulations, so the Federal pens will remain condom-free.

CHAPTER FOUR

HUMAN RELATIONS

RAINDATE

Edward: So, you have a date with Donna tonight.

Charles: She wants to take me out to dinner.

Edward: Knowing Donna, you better take your rubbers.

Charles: Heck, if it rains, I ain't going.

AH—THE MEMORIES

"It is the rare man who cannot remember slipping his very first condom into a corner of his wallet.

"Placed there at puberty, it usually remained long enough to leave a telltale ring that quietly announced he had 'arrived.' "

> —Amy Pagnozzi and Mel Jaffe,
> writers for *N.Y. Post*

"The first time I ever saw a rubber was in 8th grade, when Mikey DeJohn pulled one out of his wallet and told us he was going to use it on Debbie DeMichiel. We all went totally insane, running around screaming, 'Mikey, Mikey, Mikey's gonna do it!' at clusters of bewildered girls."

> —David Weinberg,
> writer

"I use condoms every day. I can't do it every day now. But you might say I am still on the active list."

> —Japanese businessman

"Thirty years ago, when they said they used condoms for protection, it sounded like you were going to be beaten up."

> —Dick Lord,
> comedian

"The same man that introduced me to your grandmother in 1924 also introduced me to condoms a few years earlier in Sunday school."

> —Ray Chamberlin,
> retired businessman

EXCUSE ME—ARE YOU BLUSHING?

"I always used to imagine the classic situation where you mumble to the clerk that you want a package of condoms and he turns and shouts to the guy in back, 'Hey Jimmy, one package of condoms up front!' "

—Female condom customer

"I remember as a young man going from chemist to chemist, red-faced because I was terrified of buying such an article [condom] from a female shop assistant. I finished with 15 tubes of toothpaste."

—Keith Dunstan,
an Australian

CHARGE IT

Shy about asking for condoms? Try using this at your favorite store.

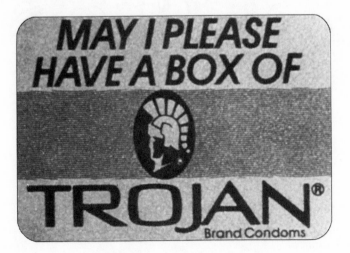

A promotion by Trojan Brand condoms

CONDOMS ARE A MAN'S BEST FRIEND

"Condoms are pretty sexy, especially when you first put them on. They are so ------ greasy that they are great. I love to put one in my wallet and walk around knowing it's in there."

—*The Intimate Male*

"She said that my wanting to use a condom meant I didn't trust her. She was so negative about it, in fact, that I started wondering if I should trust her."

—Frank,
Seattle photographer

How safe can you get? These days, I even wear a condom when I masturbate.

CONDOMS ARE A GIRL'S BEST FRIEND

"It's kind of like a security blanket."

> —Shirley Zussman,
> N.Y. sex and marital
> therapist

"My feminist political reaction is that I'm troubled by the fact that birth control remains a woman's burden and almost solely a woman's burden. My pragmatic reaction is use condoms and argue as we go along, because there is now a question of safety."

> —Letty Cottin Pogrebin,
> an editor at *Ms.* magazine

"And I've promised myself that I will get condoms before I have sex again with someone I don't know well. It's just so hard because I think there's a purpose to casual sex; it's like a drug that lets you escape the real world for a while. Who wants to attach a worry to the thing you're using to escape worry?"

> —Martha, 32-year-old
> copywriter

"I haven't had an occasion to use them; it's going to be very awkward. But I carry them in my wallet, just like a guy."

> —Jackie D'Amico, 24-year-old
> assistant to managing
> editor,
> *Penthouse* magazine

"I had to buy them. And then, to make matters worse, he refused to put it on. He said it squeezed him. We finally had sex without it, and even though I'm sure he was 'safe,' I'm still angry at myself for giving in. Next time I won't."

> —31-year-old
> research analyst

DON'T COUNT HIM OUT YET

The shapely 29-year-old married the rich 79-year-old codger and told her friends it was a football romance—she was waiting for him to kick off. Boy, was she in for a surprise when on their wedding night he emerged from the bathroom completely nude except for earplugs, nose plugs and a condom. To her obvious question he replied, " 'Cause the two things I hate the most are a woman screaming and the smell of burning rubber."

"SORRY, ELDON, I WON'T DO IT UNLESS YOU USE A CONDOM!"

THE SINGLES SCENE

"The condom is both a sexual courtesy and a sexual requirement between contemporary men and women today. What's understood is very simple. No **glove,** no love."

—Scott Hoyt,
N.Y. business executive

"I like to go dancing. I took my sisters with me one night, and, as a joke, they asked three guys to show us their condoms. My sister said, 'Condom check!' and each of these guys had one!"

—22-year-old Michigan
Brooks Brothers
saleswoman

"One guy got angry. He said, 'I won't use condoms.' He tried to make love to me, but I wouldn't let him. Stalemate."

—New York writer

"Nowadays when I meet a woman I no longer ask her birth sign, just what condom brand she uses."

—Noah Goodman,
circus performer

NOW, SET THEM UP, JOE

The Health Issues Task Force of Cleveland has taught bartenders to promote safe sex to those who might seek their advice. One can only assume barbers and taxi drivers are next.

NO LAUGHING MATTER

Attitudes in the gay community have changed radically. A study by the Schmid Company backed this up when it reported that in the 1970s, homosexuals did not use condoms. Now over 50% do.

And condom machines, once laughable in the gay community, have found their way into many gay-oriented restaurants and bars.

IS IT A BIRD? IS IT A PLANE?

No, it's Captain Condom, a muscular actor dressed in a blue outfit with a hot pink cape who, along with the Good Fairy of Safe Sex, goes into homosexual bars in Minnesota and distributes free condoms to patrons.

FASHION STATEMENT

Question: What do babies, punk rockers and homosexuals have in common?

Answer: Safety pins. They all wear them, but only the homosexuals are using them as a symbol that the individual engages only in safe sex.

TABLE TALK

". . . You must contrive, in social settings, to subtly let it be known that you have it. At a dinner party, for example, you might just happen to drop it on the floor right after the soup course has been cleared. 'Excuse me,' you would say to the people seated on either side of you, 'but I must bend over to retrieve my condom.' This would be a signal to civilized females to fawn all over this sensitive, responsible, courteous male."

—Dave Barry,
humorist

BE PREPARED

" 'Are you telling me you don't have a condom on you?' I asked, nuzzling his back and undoing his shirt. 'Well, I do,' I said, reaching down into my bag and presenting him with one. I sort of held my breath—who knew how he was going to react? But he just smiled . . ."

—Lee Ann, 27-year-old
copywriter

POETRY IN MOTION

"Even before the whole AIDS thing I was always a big believer in condoms. I made up a little poem today for my friends. I'll tell you how it went:

Don't stammer stutter
If you need a rubber
Ask Chris for a loaner
For something safe for your boner!

> —Chris, 24-year-old N.J.
> cable TV production
> assistant

CHAPTER FIVE

EDUCATION

A NEW TWIST ON YOUR ABC'S: A FOR AIDS, C FOR CONDOMS

San Francisco: Hene Kelly, a teacher at Woodrow Wilson High School, stood at the front of her classroom and put her arms around Christian Haren and Edgardo Rodriguez, two men who have AIDS.

"Are you afraid I can catch AIDS from them?" she asked the students at a recent session of her family life class.

"No," the 15- and 16-year-olds shouted back at her.

"O.K.," Ms. Kelly said. "How can you get it?"

"Sex without condoms," the class responded.

"Yeah," Ms. Kelly said. "And how else?"

"Sharing needles," came the answer.

Ms. Kelly's students, like those in similar classes in public and private high schools throughout the city, are participating in an innovative program to educate teenagers about how AIDS is transmitted.

—*New York Times,* June 1988

NURSERY RHYME

.bbers are jolly
.ubbers are fun
Better to use one
Than end up a mum!

This was the winning entry in an American competition aimed at schoolchildren to promote the condom.

U.S. SURGEON GENERAL C. EVERETT KOOP SPEAKS

"Kids aren't dumb—they know about these things. If you go to a drugstore to get a pack of gum, you'll see a box of condoms next to it."

"Nothing I ever said . . . would indicate I would ever discuss sodomy [with a child], let alone teach it . . . [And] I know a lot more about the size of an 8-year-old's penis than they do—and let me tell you, condoms don't fit."

SECRETARY OF EDUCATION WILLIAM J. BENNETT REPLIES

"Clinically correct, but morally empty."

(Comment on Koop's education policy)

Reprinted by permission of Tribune Media Services

THE REAGAN ADMINISTRATION

The Reagan administration distributed its paper on how to handle AIDS education in schools. While it does mention the possible value of condoms in preventing AIDS, the major emphasis is on "responsible sexual behavior based on fidelity, commitment, and maturity, placing sexuality within the context of marriage."

One can't help wondering if the emphasis would have changed if Gary Hart was in the White House.

THE PRESIDENT SPEAKS

"It's not how you do it but that you don't do it."
—President Reagan

Note: 20,899 Americans had died of AIDS when President Reagan gave his first speech on the topic.

THE BLACKBOARD JUNGLE

What and when to teach about AIDS and condoms is a debate raging in school districts nationwide.

The New York State Board of Regents curriculum guide swung back and forth until it landed on the conservative side—emphasizing abstinence and not mentioning condoms until the 8th grade (the original plan was 4th grade).

"How can anyone justify instructing kids in fourth grade in the use of condoms? I submit that if I had tried to do it 10 years ago I'd have been arrested as a pervert. Now it's official policy. How sad."

—Ray Kerrison,
N.Y. Post

"I am well aware discussion of condoms is an uncomfortable matter. The unhappy truth is that sexual activity occurs [among teenagers]. We must do what we can to cushion that."

—Thomas Sobol,
N.Y. State Education
Commission

FACT: In the United States one teenager (yes, a different one) becomes pregnant every 30 seconds.

BUT, OFFICER . . .

Twelve percent of high school boys surveyed claimed that due to embarrassment they stole their first condoms.

SUPERMAN, BATMAN, AND NOW . . .
VICKIE VULVA

Meet Jimmy Penis and Vickie Vulva who teach you how to use condoms in the comic book, "Condoms Are Safe," written by Don Arioli and Catherine Blake.

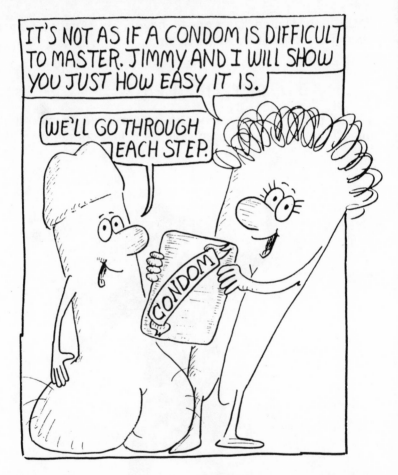

A DOLL THAT GETS AROUND

Move over, Barbie, make room for "Teach-A-Bodies," the anatomically correct dolls that come equipped with a condom, sanitary napkin, tampon, and a baby with an umbilical cord and placenta. Produced by Pediatric Projects, Inc. of Santa Monica, California, the dolls are to be used to help teach children and teenagers about sexuality and disease prevention.

IS THIS THE WAY ROCKEFELLER STARTED?

The entrepreneurial spirit is alive in Amherst, Massachusetts, where a 16-year-old student made a proposal to the school district suggesting he put condom vending machines in local junior and senior high schools. He would then split the profits with the district.

NURSERY RHYMES

In days of old
When Knights were bold
And rubber wasn't invented
They tied their socks
Around their cocks
That's how babies were prevented.

A tisket, a tasket
A condom or a casket.

If you're feeling randy
Make sure you keep a condom handy.

I ♥ NEW YORK

The New York City school system won high acclaim for an educational film on sex, drugs, and AIDS. The film ran in 48 states, but ironically, never in New York City due to a school board policy change.

"A TALE OF TWO CITIES"

The benefits of education about safe sex and condoms can be proven by "The Case of the Two Arcadias."

Due to an AIDS education program in Arcadia, Indiana, a student with AIDS was greeted enthusiastically by the high school. Conversely, three AIDS-infected hemophiliac brothers in Arcadia, Florida had their house burned down.

Was education the answer?

OVERHEARD ON DONAHUE

"If we don't educate our children in kindergarten about sex and later about condoms, we will have to get a muzzle for everyone and maybe circumcise the boys a little closer."

RAH RAH SIS BOOM BAH

There was a time college students hung pennants on their walls to show school spirit. Nowadays they can buy condoms in their school colors. Marketed by College Condoms, hundreds of these color-coordinated condoms have already been sold at U.C. Berkeley, U.S.C., U.C.L.A. and Florida State.

TO FUND OR NOT TO FUND

Many university health clinics are handing out free condoms and AIDS information, but 25% of the students polled by *Glamour* magazine claim their college health service has not yet made an organized response to AIDS.

"There's a moral question about contraception that colleges would like to avoid. If they approve of sex, it might hurt their chances of raising funds, especially at a religious school."

SCHOOL LESSONS

"I found a condom on the patio last night."

"What's a patio?"

GRADUATION GIFT

"My mother handed me two condoms on my 18th birthday. My first experience using one was with a girl named Dawn at 1:30 a.m. It happened during the same summer my mother gave them to me—thank God."

—Kevin F. Keaton,
college student

NATIONAL CONDOM WEEK

In an attempt to educate young adults about the value of condoms in controlling STDs and unwanted teen pregnancies, Mr. Fred Mayer (a Sausalito pharmacist) started National Condom Week Resource Center 10 years ago.

Beginning on Valentine's Day, colleges across the country participate in condom-related events such as a pregnant man pageant, condom water-balloon fights, and pin-the-condom-on-the-man contests. 1988 NCW sponsors: Carter Wallace, maker of Trojan condoms; Pharmacist Planning Services, Inc.; Mayer Laboratories, makers of Kimono condoms.

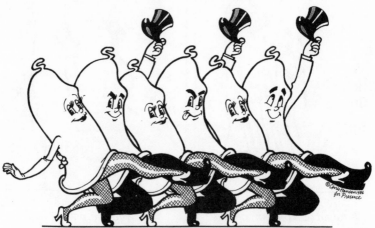

Using condoms will help stop AIDS. Get the facts. Call 800-FOR-AIDS.

SAFE SEX IS GREAT SEX.

This national condom week logo has six colorful condoms high-stepping across T-shirts, nightshirts and posters. For more information, call (415) 891-0455

RUBBER RHYMES

When moonlight glows
And nights are starry

A condom means you're never sorry.

Use a condom for your health
Protect your lover and yourself.

> —The above were entries in
> the National Condom Week
> rhymed-couplet contest.

NEW ENTRIES

A new brand of condoms to be marketed to college students is still searching for a name. Rejects so far include:

- Seaman's Choice—too gimmicky.

- Helen's Choice—average customer not familiar with Greek mythology.

- Sociables—Nabisco already grabbed that one.

WHOOPS!

The true definition of a faux pas—having Ramses sponsor the University of Southern California's football team, which is called—Trojans!

A STUDY IN CONTRASTS

In the fall of 1987, the administration at the University of Vermont allowed free condoms to be distributed via the school newspaper. Students snatched them up in minutes.

Yet, in the same week, at St. Joseph's College in the neighboring state of Maine, students aren't even allowed to visit each other in dorm rooms because "undue intimacy," says college president Dr. Loring Hart, "is not conducive to academic life."

Trojan Brand promotion in Daytona Beach (courtesy of Shapeaux Entertainment Corp.)

FIRST TIME

"My friends bought me my first condom. I told them to get ones that were lubricated. They forgot, but two hours later I realized it didn't matter. She was very wet."

—Dave Edwards,
college student

CAN YOU DELIVER THAT IN LESS THAN 20 MINUTES?

You've called up for pizza and Chinese food. Now University of Texas students can call the "Protection Connection" and have condoms and spermicidal sponges delivered to their doorsteps.

LOVE IN BLOOM

Romance is blooming on college campuses these days with couples exchanging heart-shaped boxes of condoms on Valentine's Day.

FLIP FLOPS

College men feel more comfortable purchasing condoms than college women do. Conversely, female students are more inclined to ask their partners to use one.

FLUNKING

Fifty percent of all college students think condoms come in different sizes, according to one survey.

NEED CHANGE?

Why are condom vending machines popping up on college campuses?

"Sometimes students just don't have time to get to the bookstore."

—Frank Pogue, vice
chancellor State University
of New York, Central
Administration

STUDY AIDS

Registration on some college campuses has an added bonus—safe sex kits that contain condoms and other such paraphernalia conducive to "studying."

CHAPTER SIX

LET'S GET IT ON

© 1989 Michelle Horwitz

NOT TOO BRIGHT

Did you hear about the guy who just couldn't get it right? He put ice in his condom to reduce the swelling.

REASONS TO *BAG* IT

Reasons for and advantages of using condoms.

- Most effective protection short of abstinence against sexually transmitted diseases.
- 97–99% effective if used correctly; 90–95% effective if used with average amount of care.
- Does not alter the body's chemistry.
- Requires no prescription or fitting.
- Widely available and inexpensive.
- Extremely portable and easy to hide.
- Only used when needed.
- Allows for male participation in birth control.
- No physical side effects.
- Ideally suited for a sporadic sex life.
- Could help in slowing down premature ejaculation.
- May lower the risk of cervical cancer and pelvic inflammatory disease.
- Protection against amniotic fluid infections in pregnant women.
- Safe form of birth control for nursing mothers.
- May help overcome certain types of infertility.
- Can be used along with a diaphragm for subsequent intercourse instead of more spermicidal jelly.
- Should be used during the "window period" after a vasectomy or AIDS test.

REASONS NOT TO *BAG* IT

That's right, there are no medical or health problems associated with using condoms.

That's not to say people don't have hang-ups about using rubbers. Complaints center around a lessening of sensation and the interruption of spontaneity. However, these problems can be easily solved with just one word—IMAGINATION.

By integrating condoms into your lovemaking you will find that putting them on can be just as much fun as putting it in. Additionally, when you begin to experiment with the lessons on fun ways to use a condom found in this chapter, you may find yourself so excited that a loss of sensation will never even enter your "reality."

INSERT POINT A INTO SLOT B:

STEP ONE:

Open the package carefully. Rough or jagged fingernails can damage the condom.

Helpful hint: If you put a drop of water-based lubricant inside the tip of the rubber it will give the wearer more sensation during intercourse.

Even though a condom has no moving parts, there are a few things necessary to keep in mind for them to work properly. The most important rule to remember is don't play Russian Roulette—in order to prevent unwanted pregnancies and/or the transfer of sexually transmitted diseases, condoms must be used every time there is a chance of transfer of semen to mucous membranes, i.e., vagina, rectum, or mouth.

STEP TWO:

Take hold of tip of condom, leaving approximately ½ to one inch, to allow a place for semen to go. Place over erect penis. If uncircumcised, pull back foreskin first. Then carefully roll condom all the way down the base of the shaft. Squeeze any air out of the tip and shaft of the rubbers.

Helpful Hint: This can be a one- or two-person operation. Sharing "housekeeping chores" can be fun.

It is quite possible that the condom will be longer than the penis. It is not necessary to point this out to your partner as it might deflate his ego, among other things.

STEP THREE:

Insert point A into slot B (or C, if so desired) . . .

STEP FOUR:

Before withdrawal one of you should hold the rim end of the condom so it does not slip off. Withdrawal should take place before erection subsides.

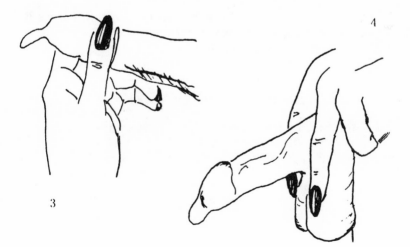

FUN WAYS TO USE A CONDOM

LESSON #1: FOUR HANDS ARE BETTER THAN TWO

Find the time to steal some magic moments.
Plan a romantic evening, set the mood.
When it's time to put the condom on—make it fun! Taking turns can help.

A woman putting a condom on a man can be a real turn-on for both partners. And this leaves his hands free to attend to other chores. Here's where your imagination spices up the action. Use it!

LESSON #2: SCIENCE PROJECT

Condoms come in a variety of types: colored, textured, lubricated, teat-ended, and some with easy-to-open packages. The only way to know which are better for you is to experiment.

Make the bedroom your laboratory as you do your own testing. Do a joint shopping trip with your partner and choose an assortment of different condoms.

Put the condom on—go ahead—feel it, taste it, caress it, check out the lube job, notice the texture, the fit . . . compare the results with your lab partner!

SLIPPERY WHEN WET

If a water-based lubricant on a condom becomes dry during sex, just put a little water on the tip and you will be "slip-sliding away . . ."

LESSON #3: PIN THE TAIL ON THE DONKEY

Bring the children's birthday game up to date—in your birthday suit! As the old proverb says, half the fun is looking for it!

TALKING HEADS

Sex is not always an easy subject to broach, and AIDS, safe sex, and contraception issues don't make it any easier. However, nothing is more important than your health and that of your partner. Therefore, it is important to know when and how to bring up the "condom question."

POPPING THE QUESTION:

Don't wait until your clothes are off and your breathing is heavy to bring up the subject of using condoms. Selecting the opportune time is key; perhaps over dinner, or during a quiet moment. The important thing is that you both be at your most relaxed.

ALLERGY PRONE

One woman who was allergic to pollen, dust and molds also found herself having allergic reactions due to having sex with a man who was taking penicillin. The solution: naturally, a condom.

The mystery here is how they figured this out.

OPENING LINES

It's not what you say, it's how you say it.

- "I'm a little nervous about bringing this up, but I think condoms make sense. What about you?"

- "Now that we've discussed how you feel about apartheid, heavy metal, gun control, and Nicaragua, what's your feeling about safe sex?"

- "I'm not planning to jump your bones right now, but I need to know how you feel about condoms before I do."

Whatever you choose to say, be confident, comfortable, patient, understanding.

Well, I thought *they would be easy to find!*

PANDORA'S BOX

Condoms don't require a large capital investment—STOCK UP!!!

Keep them convenient. In a moment of passion no one wants to hike to the bathroom or rummage through the sock drawer. A small decorative box filled with condoms and kept in reaching distance of the bed could prove to be a lifesaver.

POINT: COUNTERPOINT

When bringing up safe sex and condoms, you must be prepared for all types of answers.

POINT	COUNTERPOINT
"I'm not diseased."	"No, I don't believe I am either, but I'm not sure about the gorilla I made love to yesterday!"
"It's like taking a shower with your raincoat on!"	"Whatever we lose in sensation, we'll make up for with imagination!"
"Just this once."	"Once is all it takes."

Whatever the response, don't overreact. Remember, it's just your partner's initial reaction. Face it with love and understanding, but most importantly, be firm. This is a matter of life and death—literally. Be confident that you are protecting yourself and your partner.

THE ANSWER TO ALL YOUR QUESTIONS

Q: I am worried about contracting a venereal disease during sex. What should I do? Also, I suffer from premature ejaculation. Any suggestions? And finally, I would like to increase the size of my penis. What do you recommend?

A: 1. Wear a condom. 2. Wear two condoms. 3. Wear three condoms.

—Playboy magazine

LESSON #4: SMOOTH TALK

We all love those stockings and garter belts in sheer and madly sensuous fabrics. Here's an erotic touch that will make condom use an extra turn-on . . .

. . . Place hand in stocking (try not to tear). Using the hand covered with the fabric, carefully unroll the condom onto the penis.

Let the length of the stocking rub against the man's naked body—all parts are fair game.

Add a few extra sensuous strokes to keep the passion moving.

After you've finished rubbing your man's body with your silks and satins, choose your most erotic position to teasingly put on your stockings for the culminating act.

LESSON #5: DOUBLE YOUR PLEASURE

Try double-bagging it.

Believe it or not, many claim wearing two condoms feels better than one because of the friction they help create.

LESSON #6: HOLIDAY CHEER

Looking for a present that's unique? How about a condom grab bag—a festive pouch filled with a variety of condoms and plans to attempt to use them all. Happy whatever!

A LAST RESORT

If you can't come to an agreement on using a condom, you need to make some difficult decisions.

There *are* ways to enjoy yourself without exchanging bodily fluids. Old stand-bys such as hugging, petting, mutual masturbation and what used to be called "grinding" can still be fun.

Another alternative is to give him/her up—if they don't care enough about your health or their own they may not prove to be a good choice in partners.

TIE A RIBBON ROUND THE OLD OAK TREE

It's not how long you are, it's how long you make it last. If you suffer from premature ejaculation, condoms can help to slow you down by creating a slight tourniquet effect. Adding a second condom tied around the base, or a cock ring, can also serve the purpose.

HEALTH NOTICE

Since no one really knows how long the AIDS virus lives outside the body, it might not be a bad idea to wash up afterwards. And, to save water, try showering with your lover.

LESSON #7: THE MALE STRIPPER

Turn down the lights, choose music to set the mood, get comfortable and let the stripper take his position on the stage. Slowly and erotically let the strip begin.

Take your time—enjoy yourself.

When all the clothes are off, it's time for the second act. As erotically as he undressed, he should re-dress with just one item—a condom. The climax of the show is in your hands.

LESSON #8 FAIRY TALES CAN COME TRUE

Sometimes it's fun to escape into fantasy, and it can heighten the illusion to incorporate a condom into the make-believe. If you don't have a favorite fantasy, here are a few scenarios:

• The fastidious French maid. She must make sure everything (condom included) is in its proper place.

• The condom salesperson who is more than willing to ensure a perfect fit—personally.

• How about playing doctor? He wears a rubber **glove**—but it's not on his hand . . .

YOU CAN'T GO TO MIDAS FOR A LUBE JOB

Extra lubrication will add to the sensation and will give you extra security against condom breakage.

However, oil-based petroleum jelly and alcohol lubricants can cut the strength of the condom in half, so be careful about what you're greasing up with.

SUGGESTED LUBRICANTS

- Water-soluble lubricants

- K-Y jelly®

- Spermicidal foam & jelly

- H-R lubricating jelly®

- Surgilube®

NO-NO'S

- Oil-based lubricants

- Any lubricants containing alcohol

- Petroleum jelly

- Cold Cream

- Vegetable shortening

- Baby oil

- Mineral oil

- Massage oil

- Butter

- Most hand creams

LESSON #9: NOW FOR THE SWEET STUFF

For those who value oral gratification, you can always enhance the taste of a condom with your favorite topping, like honey, whipped cream, or chocolate syrup. Change condoms before intercourse.

Remember though, don't use anything with alcohol or oil.

LESSON #10: PLANNING THE PERFECT WEEKEND

Everyone loves a romantic holiday. But we always pack too much . . . and probably not enough! Next time only pack what you need—candles, condoms, hot lingerie, condoms, cold wine, condoms . . . have fun!

LESSON #11: ALL TIED UP

Ingredients:

1. Scarves, ties, cloth belts, feather optional.
2. Several condoms.
3. Imagination!

Tie the man up.

Then, tease, tease, tease . . . here's where the feather can come in handy.

When it is obvious he is starting to take a "hard line" attitude, put a condom on him.

Make believe you're going to take things further along, and then change your mind.

Remove condom.

Repeat procedure. Condoms are cheap. (But *not* reusable!)

Don't be surprised if this scenario reaches its climax sooner than you thought!

SERVE AT ROOM TEMPERATURE

Keep condoms away from heat sources (exception: body heat), and out of the glove compartment. Don't keep them in your wallet for too long. Condoms should last three to five years from the date of manufacture.

"Now I have absolutely nothing to worry about except the Trojan [Brand condom] I have been carrying around so long in my wallet that inside its tinfoil wrapper it has probably been half eaten away by mold. One spurt and the whole thing will go flying in pieces all over the inside of Bubbles Giardi's box—and *then* what will I do?"

—Philip Roth
Portnoy's Complaint

FREUD SAID THERE ARE NO ACCIDENTS—BUT WHAT DID HE KNOW?

What to do in case semen leaks into the vagina? As the Boy Scouts say: be prepared—have a spermicidal jelly, cream or foam on hand to use right away. In extreme cases there is the post-coital hormonal contraceptive (morning-after pill). But remember, don't douche. It might make matters worse.

LESSON #12 PARTY TRICKS

It's always fun to have a unique talent, such as knowing how to separate egg whites, or being a jacks champion, or even flipping baseball cards.

Another skill might be acquiring the ability to put a condom on an erect penis using only your mouth. The goal, for safety reasons, is to put your mouth only on the rubber, not on the penis. Since practice makes perfect, why not try the trick on a banana first?

Just a second, honey. Try to hold the mood!

PURCHASING POWER

And whose responsibility is it to make sure your condom supply is stocked? BOTH PARTIES'. Today it is socially acceptable for women to buy and carry their own condoms.

Gone are the days when prophylactics were hidden under the counter. In many states today, they are on open display right next to the baby diapers.

THE RUBBER SLIPPER

At last my search is over! I found the perfect fit.

PITFALLS

How to avoid the most common causes of condom failure:

Don't suffer from "just this once" syndrome. Most condom failures are caused by lack of use.

If you've had a condom in your wallet for a long time, consider yourself unlucky. Throw it out, buy some new ones and hope your luck changes.

The one thing you should not throw in the wash is condoms. Only use them once.

Sometimes the best defense is knowing when to withdraw—pull out before the erection is lost.

LESSON #13: THE GRAND PRIX (FOR MEN ONLY)

A race to the finish.
   Get ready, get set—GO!
   It's not hard to figure out. The object of the race is to get the condom in place first. Winner gets to choose his prize.

HEALTH NOTICE

Natural lambskin condoms may have a different permeability than latex and may not lend themselves to the same degree of uniformity in manufacture as synthetic materials such as latex. In the interest of prudence, therefore, the FDA requests that natural lambskin condoms not be labeled "for protection against STDs."

CHAPTER SEVEN

RX: PRESCRIPTION FOR LOVE

GOOD OLD DAYS

"I don't believe Doc Fiedler is still with us, but if he is, he doesn't have to worry about putting Trojans [Brand condoms] under the counter anymore. You can have a nice big display in your store window, and no one could care less. . . . The fun of buying them was sneaking to the back of the store and making my purchase before anyone caught me. What's the big deal of showing off to my friends when they can see them for themselves right next to the L'eggs display by the door?"

—Art Buchwald,
humorist

BEST FRIENDS

"The pharmacist and I are best friends now. Every time a new brand comes in, he tells me about them."

—37-year-old businesswoman

AND NOW A WORD FROM YOUR LOCAL DRUGGIST

"Pharmacists aren't shocked by anything, so don't feel you have to wear a disguise when buying condoms."

—Russell Friedman,
Philadelphia pharmacist

"Hey, there's a guy here wants some information on Trojans"

Well, sure.

Most men would like to know more about Trojan® brand condoms.

But they're seriously afraid of suffering a spectacular and terminal attack of embarrassment right in the middle of a well-lighted drugstore.

In fact, there's no reason for this sort of panic. Most drugstores now provide a convenient self-service rack, where you'll find the whole range of Trojan condoms. (Along with noticeably unembarrassed consumers making their selections.)

But why wait till you get to the drugstore? We herewith offer information on the various different forms of Trojan available.

TO MAKE THE RIGHT CHOICE,
YOU'VE GOT TO KNOW WHAT THE CHOICES ARE.

First, you should know in what ways Trojan condoms are all alike.

Every Trojan condom is a mere 0.003 of an inch thin. And ultrasensitive. (We're almost as dedicated to your pleasure as you are.)

Every Trojan condom is also highly effective in preventing pregnancy. (Did you know the condom is the most effective form of birth control available without a prescription? It's true.)

And all Trojan condoms, when you use them properly, can help reduce the risk of spreading many sexually transmitted diseases. (Your doctor can tell you more.)

So every man should probably consider using Trojan condoms. But not every man should consider the same kind. Which brings us to the different kinds available.

TROJANS.® The classic, round end, unlubricated condom. Highly effective birth control, without frills.

TROJAN-ENZ.® Unlubricated, with a reservoir tip.

TROJAN-ENZ® LUBRICATED: The reservoir tip, plus lubrication to make everything a bit easier.

TROJAN PLUS.® The feeling of a form-fitting condom, the pleasure of a special "whisper-light" lubricant, and the special look of gold color.

TROJAN® RIBBED: For your partner's special pleasure, delicately textured ribs. For the pleasure of both of you, "whisper-light" lubricant, transparency, and gold color.

TROJAN NATURALUBE® Natural "jelly" type lubrication, partner-pleasing ribs, reservoir tip, and form-fitting shape.

Okay. We've given you the descriptions. Now comes your part.

Experiment a little. Try the various kinds of Trojan condoms. That way, you'll be sure you know which is the right one for you. And knowledge is, as they say, power.

But in this case it's pleasure, too.

| TROJANS | TROJAN-ENZ | TROJAN-ENZ LUBRICATED | TROJAN PLUS | TROJAN RIBBED | TROJAN NATURALUBE |

TROJAN® CONDOMS
BRAND
For all the right reasons.

© 1986 Carter-Wallace, Inc.

75

FOR PREVENTION OF VENEREAL DISEASES

Correct Way To Use Mechanical (Rubber) Prophylactics

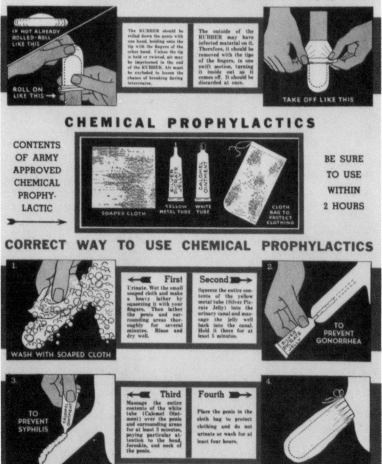

IF NOT ALREADY ROLLED—ROLL LIKE THIS

ROLL ON LIKE THIS →

The RUBBER should be rolled down the penis with one hand, holding onto the tip with the fingers of the other hand. Unless the tip is held or twisted, air may be imprisoned in the end of the RUBBER. Air must be excluded to lessen the chance of breaking during intercourse.

The outside of the RUBBER may have infected material on it. Therefore, it should be removed with the tips of the fingers, in one swift motion, turning it inside out as it comes off. It should be discarded at once.

TAKE OFF LIKE THIS

CHEMICAL PROPHYLACTICS

CONTENTS OF ARMY APPROVED CHEMICAL PROPHYLACTIC
→

SOAPED CLOTH

SILVER PICRATE JELLY
YELLOW METAL TUBE

CALOMEL OINTMENT
WHITE TUBE

CLOTH BAG TO PROTECT CLOTHING

BE SURE TO USE WITHIN 2 HOURS

CORRECT WAY TO USE CHEMICAL PROPHYLACTICS

1. WASH WITH SOAPED CLOTH

←— First
Urinate. Wet the small soaped cloth and make a heavy lather by squeezing it with your fingers. Then lather the penis and surrounding areas thoroughly for several minutes. Rinse and dry well.

Second ■■■→
Squeeze the entire contents of the yellow metal tube (Silver Picrate Jelly) into the urinary canal and massage the jelly well back into the canal. Hold it there for at least 5 minutes.

2. TO PREVENT GONORRHEA

3. TO PREVENT SYPHILIS

←— Third
Massage the entire contents of the white tube (Calomel Ointment) over the penis and surrounding areas for at least 3 minutes, paying particular attention to the head, foreskin, and neck of the penis.

Fourth ■■■→
Place the penis in the cloth bag to protect clothing and do not urinate or wash for at least four hours.

4. TO PROTECT CLOTHING

DOCTORS' ADVICE

"I believe a properly used condom is an effective preventive measure against AIDS as well as other STDs. But, an improperly used one is worse, because it encourages injudicious, and potentially very dangerous, sexual behavior."

—Dr. Cecil Fox, senior
scientist at the National
Institute of Health

"Women should be encouraged to practice putting a condom on a cucumber, for example, and not only to handle it but also to smell and taste it. Men should be encouraged to masturbate while wearing a condom."

—Dr. Martha Gross,
Washington D.C.,
psychologist

"If you think you might face a shortage, bring them [condoms] along, just like you would your soap or toothpaste."

—Dr. James Chin, AIDS
expert at W.H.O. talking to
travelers

OPTIMIST

Man buys twelve packs of condoms on Friday. On Monday he is back in the drugstore complaining that he was only given eleven.

The druggist looks at him and shrugs. "Sorry. Did I spoil your weekend?"

THE ODDS ARE . . .

"There are a minimum of 10 million STDs recorded annually. Which means that about every 5 seconds an American is involved in a high risk sexual practice minus a condom."

—Dr. German Maisonet,
medical director L.A.
Minority AIDS Project

"Someone who has had one or two sexual encounters without using a condom is at much greater risk than someone who has had 10 or 20 and used a condom every time."

—John Graves,
program director American
Social Health Association

HOLE IN ONE

First Nurse: "I fixed the doctor—I broke all his thermometers."

Second Nurse: "That's nothing compared to what I did to that S.O.B. I put holes in all his condoms."

Third Nurse: Faints dead away.

CHAPTER EIGHT

FAMOUS FACES

"First we roll out the TV ads, and then he becomes a beloved character on the Saturday-morning cartoon shows!"

Reproduced by Special Permission of Playboy Magazine: Copyright © 1987 by Playboy

CONDOMS ABOUT TOWN

. . . Former boxer Tony Danza (WHO'S THE BOSS, TAXI) is helping to fight the battle against AIDS through public service spots that encourage teenagers to use condoms during sex . . .

. . . Rebecca Holden (GENERAL HOSPITAL) is now dispensing information as spokesperson for Safe-Con: condoms by mail. They are expensive, but there is always a surcharge for privacy. . .

. . . Spotted at New York's trendy Club Paradise, Holly Gagnaia (Cassie on ONE LIFE TO LIVE) was not only dancing, but also handing out hand-painted boxes of Lifestyle brand condoms! It's the only way, really . . .

. . . Chynna Phillips, daughter of Michelle Phillips of the Mamas and the Papas, is growing up. She says her mom keeps a drawerful of condoms, foams, and sponges for herself and her pals who may need such things . . .

. . . A certain SATURDAY NIGHT LIVE anchorman is dedicated to his work. In a recent show, he wore a body condom. "I'll do a lot for the news," he said, "But I won't die for it." . . .

. . . Ronnie Reagan, Jr., dangled a prophylactic on the PBS special AIDS: CHANGING THE RULES, as he spoke the line, "This is a condom." . . .

. . . For movie buffs: What flicks mention condoms? A starter list—SUMMER OF '42, TWO MOON JUNCTION, MYSTIC PIZZA, THE KISS, DRAGNET, BROADCAST NEWS, YOU CAN'T HURRY LOVE, BACHELOR PARTY . . .

AND ON THE SILVER SCREEN

In DRAGNET (the movie), Tom Hanks gives up on a morning quickie when he realizes he is out of condoms.

In BROADCAST NEWS, to prepare for a hot date with William Hurt, Holly Hunter brings along a package of Trojan Brand Condoms—wouldn't you?!

Elisa Florez, star of the X-rated GREEN DOOR: THE SEQUEL (and former staff member for a U.S. senator), insisted that each of her partners wear two condoms in case one broke. When they realized that two created friction, no complaints were heard on the set.

Walt Disney Productions has released a safe-sex educational film that features Ally Sheedy and promotes the use of condoms.

NOT WITH MY BANANA

Panamanian superstar Ruben Blades, appearing in the PBS special AIDS: CHANGING THE RULES, showed viewers how to use a condom by dressing a banana in one.

As you know, you can't please everyone, and the head of the Banana Association sent a letter of complaint, claiming the banana is an "important fruit and deserves to be treated with respect." They may have a point, but one should not have sex with an unprotected banana.

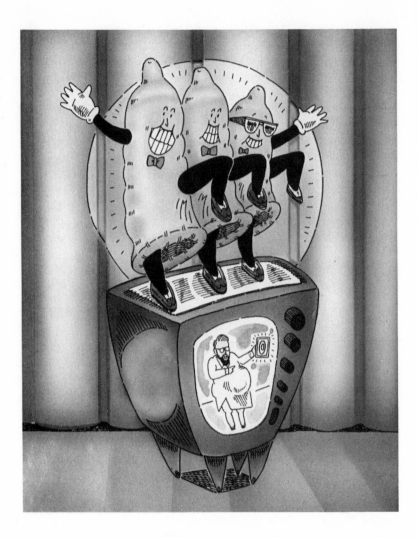

CONDOMS ON TV

On ST. ELSEWHERE they talk about an unmarried pregnant woman who should have had her lover "condomized."

Additionally, CAGNEY & LACEY, KATE & ALLIE, FACTS OF LIFE, VALERIE, and the daytime soap DAYS OF OUR LIVES have all taken part in trying to help promote safe sex through condom usage.

"Protection, responsibility . . . condoms, Harve."
> —Mary Beth Lacey to husband on CAGNEY & LACEY

"Just make sure whatever you do, it's the right time in your life."
> —Valerie, upon finding her son's package of condoms

SAFETY SHEATH

"We on the LATE SHOW want to promote safe driving so if you're driving home—wear a condom."
> —David Letterman, March 1988

THE COSMOPOLITAN RAINCOAT

"You can't tell a man is wearing one when he makes love to you. A condom does not spoil his pleasure. Yes, he possibly has to stop near the peak of excitement to get it on, but this little **raincoat** does not keep him from having an orgasm."
> —Helen Gurley Brown, publisher of *Cosmopolitan* magazine

ADVICE COLUMN

"We must let condoms be dispensed in an ethical, moral way, in good taste. Not just say, 'Here are condoms.' "

—Dr. Ruth Westheimer

"Practice safe sex, by safe sex I mean protect your partner by using condoms."

—Ann Landers

"Heterosexual men should carry and be prepared to wear a condom on request."

—Xaviera Hollander

CHAPTER NINE

AROUND THE WORLD

THE CONDOM EQUATOR

"I determined that if a rubber is about seven inches long, my government bought 82,860 miles' worth. Tied together, they would wrap around the world three times and enough would be left over to make a bow that, if draped over the Horn of Africa, would reach from Madagascar to Sri Lanka."

—Robert Coran
on government issuing
condoms as aid to Third
World

HEY, BIG SPENDER

On the planet Earth over 4 billion condoms are used per year. But who is the biggest single purchaser?

Ronald Reagan.

From 1981 to 1987, the U.S. government, under the auspices of A.I.D. (Agency for International Development) sent 2.6 billion condoms to 70 countries.

BUT DON'T HAVE FUN

The A.I.D. program sends colored, light bulb–shaped and extra-thin condoms overseas but not textured ones, because:

"You can go only so far because of politics. Having fun is out. If Senator Helms thought that somebody was having fun with what we do, we'd be dead."

—anonymous A.I.D. worker

OFF-COLOR

Some American men might like to use green condoms and pretend they're Martians landing, but A.I.D. knows not to ship green condoms to Moslem countries. The color is sacred.

AFTER-DINNER MINTS

A restaurant in Denmark started to hand out condoms instead of mints as a public service to the community.

COCAINE ENCHILADAS

On September 12, 1987, a man checked into a New York City hospital complaining of severe abdominal pain and constipation. The diagnosis—46 condoms stuffed with cocaine that he had swallowed in order to smuggle the drug out of Colombia.

HOTEL GIFTS

The four-star Shangri-La Hotel, Montreal, was the first to add condoms to the toiletries left in the guest rooms.

However, a hotel in Gillette, Montana, supplied free condoms under different circumstances. When the McMullins turned down their hotel bed, they found used condoms. What type of tip do you think they left the maid?

SAM, YOU'VE MADE THE PANTS TOO LONG

The shortest teat-ended American condom is too long to comply with Hungarian government standards.

The author, whose husband is Hungarian, finds this fact a bit hard to swallow.

A Thailand newspaper editorial complained that the condoms distributed by the American A.I.D. organization "couldn't be kept in place and a string had to be used to tie them to the waist."

COPS AND RUBBERS

Ask for a Mechai in Thailand, and you'll get a box of condoms. Mechai Viravaitaya (whose calling card is a pack of condoms) runs a population program called Cops and Rubbers.

In addition to having monks bless condom shipments, and having politicians stage televised condom-inflating contests, Mechai makes condom usage fun by having C.C.C.D.—Color Coordinated Condom Days—red on Sundays, yellow on Mondays, black when in mourning . . .

FLYING CONDOMS

Tonight 107 Swedes will get gonorrhea. Do you use the condom?

In Sweden in the early '70s the above ad, which features a flying condom, was part of a campaign that helped bring about an 80% drop in gonorrhea cases.

LESSON #1

In India, a family planning worker gave instructions on how to use condoms, by placing them over a stick. One poor farmer complained that his wife became pregnant even though he put the condom on a stick every night.

SINGLE(S)

One letter can make a lot of difference. In India each condom package states "For Single Use Only." Not at all the same as "For Singles Use Only"!

POWER TO THE SEMEN

In India, Bangladesh, and Sri Lanka, many believe that a woman gets her strength from her husband's semen. Therefore, if a wife used a condom, she would not receive her husband's power.

LUCKY SHEEP

What do Americans import from New Zealand besides kiwi? The caecum (a part of the intestines) of sheep—for producing natural skin condoms. It's one condom per caecum.

YOU CAN LEARN A FEW THINGS FROM THESE DUMMIES

In Third World countries, plays utilizing puppets are often used to educate the population about birth control . . .

THE CONDOM

Arjun: Look! Supposing I plant a seed. Like this. (Arjun plants a seed. He pats down the earth and gets a watering jar and pours some water. Up comes the plant.)

Lal: That's just what happens to me. I plant the seed and I get a new baby.

Arjun: Look here. This is one way to limit your family. Now remember when I planted the corn . . .

Lal: And it popped right up? (Arjun takes seed again and wraps it up. Plants it.)

Arjun: Ah, but watch! I've wrapped up the seed—it can't get out. See, the seed can't get out. (He pats it down. Waters it. They both bend over the place in the ground and look at it, then at each other.)

Lal: All wrapped up, eh? Can't get out, no?

Arjun: No!

Lal: No plant.

Arjun: No baby.

Lal: No baby—it's like that?

Arjun: You can do the same thing too by wrapping up your seed. There is a wrapper a man wears when he is making love. Many men are using it all over the world.

FACTS AND NOTHING BUT THE FACTS FROM ENGLAND

Studies show that when couples find themselves in bed for the first time, 70% use **Johnnies**.

Durex condom, the leading brand in England, asked the public what they wanted in a condom. The answer, which is now being sold: A tinted gold 9-inch blunt-ended condom, one inch longer than the regular.

When Richard Bransen, the owner of Virgin Records, started Mates Condoms (all profits go to AIDS research) he urged his record artists to compose songs about safe sex.

DIPLOMATIC MISSION

To get even with his Russian counterpart who was always bragging about things Russian, an American businessman made up 15-inch-long condoms and sent them over in a box marked "Small."

THE YIN & THE YANG OF IT ALL

Japan is the largest user of condoms in the world, with 75% of all couples partaking in condomized sex.

Deep-rooted cultural abhorrence to altering the body's harmony, dislike of foreign objects in their bodies, and traditional taste in sex objects are some of the reasons why condoms are so popular with the Japanese.

SAMURAI CONDOMS

They say the Japanese have a larger selection of condoms than Burpee has cucumber seeds. There is a variety of colors, shapes and thicknesses, ones that are scented, and others that are embossed with flowers.

In the '60s, black was a favorite color of condoms, but these days tastes run to pastels. For reasons unknown, psychedelic ones were banned by the government.

The Japanese sure know how to **bag** it! They put condoms in boxes that are so ornate, foreigners have bought them thinking they were chocolates. For convenience, they also put in disposable bags and towelets. And though we can only guess at the tune, condoms can also be purchased in music boxes.

A Japanese twist on the Avon Lady is the "Skins Lady." They sell condoms door-to-door and make quite a lot of money doing it.

Condoms are so integrated into Japanese life that supermarkets even run specials on them.

IF IT WASN'T FOR THE AIR FARE

In Korea and China, condoms sell for between $11 and $12 a gross. Now, if toothpaste and soap were that cheap it might pay to take a trip.

PICK YOUR PLEASURE

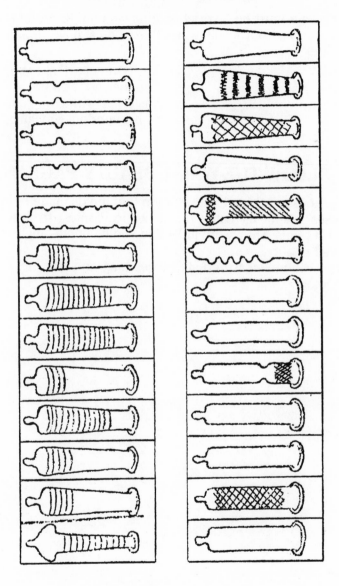

Selections from a Japanese sales catalog that shows over two dozen varieties.

A ROSE BY ANY OTHER NAME

"Your wife must be a very beautiful woman. Beautiful roses
have thorns. Your lovely wife's thorns must have ripped the
condom."

> —Mr. Okamoto, Fuji Latex
> Founder, to an irate
> customer who complained
> of his condom breaking.

A BELOW-THE-WAIST BEAUTY PAGEANT

Two thousand three hundred men had molds made of their
penises when Fuji Latex ran a beauty contest to find the
perfect penis. They were judged in width, length, angle, and
overall beauty.

The winner measured six inches long and two inches in
diameter.

CHAPTER TEN

ADVERTISING

We met the challenge! Of 100 brands of condoms surveyed in a 24-hour endurance test, we find Brand X to be longer lasting, more satisfying, and better-tasting than the leading brand. . . .

THE KOOPS

"Advertising condoms in a tasteful way is a lot different than throwing them from a Mardi Gras float in New Orleans."

—C. Everett Koop,
U.S. Surgeon General

"Well, I'm glad your mother's dead."

—Mrs. Koop to her husband
on the morning he was to
testify to Congress in favor
of condom advertising

THE LONG HARD ROAD OF CONDOM ADVERTISING

Prior to the 1970s, the law stated that condoms were allowed to be advertised as protection against venereal disease, but could not be advertised for contraceptive purposes. Consequently, condom ads were only seen in girlie magazines.

Even Playboy rejected condom ads because the magazine felt such ads would "disturb the euphoria of our readers."

The attitude changes brought on by the late '60s sexual revolution and a rise in venereal disease fanned a spurt of legitimate advertising. But parochial views once again reigned, and condom ads quietly slipped away.

It took another sixteen years to get condom advertising out from under the covers. What changed the media's attitude toward condom advertising? In a word—AIDS.

SAFE SEX FOR HIRE

Screw magazine, with its plethora of ads for all kinds of "sex for hire," now has ads showing sexy ladies holding a package of condoms, claiming theirs is the safest house in town.

"Someone I respect
has been urging me to
use condoms.
He's the Surgeon General."

"I've heard what the
Surgeon General is saying
about condoms.
And believe me, I'm listening."

The makers of Trojan latex condoms would like you to know that there are really only two ways to be absolutely sure of safety regarding sex.

One is a faithful marriage to a healthy person.

And the other is abstinence.

In all other cases, as the Surgeon General of the United States says, "An individual must be warned to use the protection of a condom."

Trojan latex condoms, America's most widely used and trusted brand, help reduce the risk of spreading many sexually transmitted diseases.

We urge you to use them in any situation where there is any possibility of sexually transmitted disease.

Look at it this way. You have nothing to lose. And what you stand to save is your life.

TROJAN
BRAND LATEX CONDOMS
For all the right reasons.

FAMOUS FIRST

1969 *Sport* magazine was the first consumer magazine to run a condom ad. In those puritanical days, while it spoke of V.D. prevention, it never once mentioned condoms.

1970 The first major newspaper to run a condom ad (the advertiser was Julius Schmid, Inc.) was the San Francisco *Chronicle.* Headline: "How Many of Your Children Did You Really Want?"

1975 After a local California T.V. station ran the first condom ad (Trojan Brand), the switchboard was inundated with calls. Not sure whether to continue this campaign, they put the ad on the evening news and solicited viewers' opinions. The vote was overwhelmingly in favor of keeping it on. But in the end, the station decided not to air the commercials.

1985 While filming what was to become the first condom commercial to air on cable, Dr. Ruth, who was Lifestyle Brand condoms spokesperson, insisted all crew members take home samples.

1987 For Memorial Day, the Boston *Phoenix* gave its readers more than the news—it became the first consumer newspaper to give away samples of condoms. The product was supplied by the makers of Trojan Brand condoms.

1987 It took another twelve years and the AIDS dilemma until the next station, KRON in San Francisco, ran a condom ad (Trojan Brand) on television.
However, there were stipulations: the manufacturer had to match money for airtime with donations to AIDS research (KRON did the same with revenue), the ad couldn't run on children's programming, and the message had to focus on disease prevention and could not mention birth control.

AD COPY:

Man: I'm 24, single, and worried. I'm a nice guy. I go out with nice girls. But these days, some pretty terrible things are happening to some pretty nice people.

L.A. County Medical Association was the first medical association to utilize billboards to promote safe sex.

THE FIRST STILL MISSING

The three networks (with an estimated 9,000 scenes of suggested sexual intercourse in a given year) feel they are defending the moral fabric of our society by not allowing condom advertising on their airwaves.

EROTIC ART

"Color is a powerful sexual stimulus. In ancient civilizations, experienced women excited their partners by painting their vulvas in the lush colors of the natural surroundings.

"Tahiti lets you excite your partner with condoms that are Morning Blue, Sunset Gold . . . Colors—Dawn Pink, Siesta Green, Midnight Black, and Black Cat for the bold."

—Tahiti condoms ad

ATTENTION, PHARMACISTS!

1927—First trade ads directed at druggists

POINT: COUNTERPOINT

"The routine promotion of condoms through advertising has been stopped by networks who are so hypocritically priggish that they refuse to describe disease control as they promote disease transmission."

—Rep. Henry Waxman
(D-Calif.)

"Kids wear T-shirts with jackets to look like Don Johnson. If he said he used birth control, on T.V., they would use it, too."

—Boy from South Bronx

"Clearly, the advertising of contraceptives is an issue that deals with many social, religious, and ethical considerations . . . a significant portion of our audience finds these products inappropriate for advertising in a medium with such powerful reach into American homes."

—ABC spokesperson

WHEN, NETWORKS, WHEN?

"Television networks will not broadcast advertisements for contraceptives until men have babies, a woman runs a network, or the president of a network gets AIDS."

—Linda Ellerbee,
host and writer for
ABC-TV's OUR WORLD

However, condoms have become the darling of the morning talk show:
"Six months ago, the networks would bleep us if we used the word condom. But more recently [January '87], when I went on the TODAY show, it was 'no problem.'"

—Judith Cohen
(runs Project Aware, an
outreach program for San
Francisco women at risk)

ADVICE STATESIDE

"When J.R. took Mandy for a roll in the hay, which one had the condom?"

> —Planned Parenthood
> Federation of America, Inc.

"Our shoes aren't the only things we encourage you to wear."

> —Kenneth Cole Shoes
> public service ad

"Very often, the best contraceptive for a woman is the one for a man."

> —Trojan Brand condoms

"They make a fantastic gift for that special occasion when words . . . just aren't enough."

> —Planned Parenthood,
> San Francisco

"Menswear for Women."

> —Lifestyle Brand condoms

"And if he says no, so can you."

> —U.S. Dept. of Health

". . . you live in a world I never imagined . . . with herpes and AIDS and a whole list of scary diseases . . . I can't even pronounce. This is a gift of love and caring, and I hope, understanding."

> —Ramses Extra Brand
> condoms

"I think it's cute! Just what a condom jingle should be!"

ADVICE FROM ABROAD

Spokesperson: Wicked Willie (a stylized penis with an attitude toward life similar to that of Garfield the cat).

Message: "Be a clever dick—protect yourself against AIDS."

—public service ad, England

Tag line: "So tell him, if it's not on, it's all off."

—Sweden

Visual: The "I" of "AIDS" makes advances on a neighbor, but it is rebuffed until it puts on a condom.

—public service ad, Norway

Tag line: "Real men do it in a Jiffi."

—Jiffi condoms, England

Headline: "Mates takes the worry out of whoopie."

—Mates condoms, England
(trial ad)

Visual: A parked car that is shaking, implying the presence of a couple in the back seat.

Tag line: "Durex Condoms. For those moments when you forget everything else."

—Durex condoms in France

A STEP IN THE RIGHT DIRECTION

Though they do not accept brand-specific condom advertising, in 1988 the networks started airing public service announcements that promoted condoms as protection against the deadly AIDS virus.

"Very often, the best contraceptive for a woman is the one for a man."

"Okay. What would be the best contraceptive for a woman?

First of all, and obviously, it would be highly reliable. (Worrying about unintended pregnancy may be the quickest way of destroying pleasure known to woman.)

Second, it should be without the serious side effects that can occur with some forms of birth control.

Then, it should also be available without a prescription. Not complicated to buy—or to use, for that matter.

And if it could help provide some protection against many sexually transmitted diseases, wouldn't that be wonderful.

And ideally (let's tell it like it is), this form of contraception would be a male-female shared responsibility.

Get ready for a little surprise. This contraceptive exists.

It's the Trojan condom.

Condoms are highly reliable and effective.

Use them properly, and they're the most effective form of birth control you can buy without a prescription.

They're completely without serious side effects and won't interfere with the way nature intended your body to work.

They're easy to buy—you'll find them in any drugstore, usually on a display rack.

(You may also find that when your partner regards contraception as his responsibility, too, it can bring a very special, sharing quality to your relationship.)

But there's even more. The condom helps reduce the risk of spreading many sexually transmitted diseases.

It's easy to see why a woman would like the idea of condoms as a contraceptive. Now, why Trojan condoms?

Because the Trojan brand is highly respected, widely trusted, and the one that's used the most.

So if you're interested in a form of contraception that benefits women, it's simple. Just consider the one for a man."

TROJAN®
BRAND CONDOMS

For all the right reasons.

Sensitivity, strength, security, intelligence. All the qualities women look for in a man can also be found in a foilpack of condoms.

They're an extremely effective way to prevent pregnancy. Especially when they're used with contraceptive foam.

They're fun to put on, if you use your imagination.

And they make a fantastic gift for that special occasion when words... just aren't enough.

You can get them at any drugstore or your local Planned Parenthood.

So next time, show how much you care. With foam for her. And condoms for you.

It might take a sense of humor. But it's part of getting serious.

Planned Parenthood®
Federation of America

810 Seventh Avenue
New York, NY 10019

Protect your love with condoms.

106

AND NOW A LITTLE SIDESTEP

New York City was the first city to run a television campaign promoting condoms for safe sex.

Scene: Condom coming out of a woman's purse.

Tag line: "Don't go out without your rubbers."

Mayor Koch stood solidly behind the campaign—sometimes.

"Condoms will not allow the virus to be transmitted. Use common sense. Protect yourself. Use condoms."

—Ed Koch, Mayor
February 22, 1987

"Using condoms to avoid AIDS is playing Russian roulette because they don't always work."

—Ed Koch
June 8, 1987

"I am 100% for condom advertising. That doesn't mean I can't be 100% for additional ads which would promote abstinence."

—Ed Koch
June 9, 1987

BOWLING AIN'T WHAT IT USED TO BE

AIDS has had strange side effects on many businesses, but the strangest might have been on Australian bowling alleys. A government public service spot showed the Grim Reaper bowling down the tenpins of frightened men, women and children.

The campaign was supposed to show how anyone can be infected with AIDS. Instead, many got the impression that bowling alleys are breeding grounds for the virus, and alley attendance dropped off.

A SENSATIONAL FEELING

Japanese regulations state that surface irregularity should not be pronounced enough to produce increased sensation, but just the idea of it. But that didn't stop one maker from using the following ad:

"More Big or Rubber Band: This may be used by men who have small tools in order to increase sexual pleasure which gives unexplainable feeling to women."

CHAPTER ELEVEN

BUSINESS AS USUAL

A MILLION-DOLLAR IDEA

When he first decided to get into the condom business, he worried about whether he would be invited anywhere. So he bounced his idea off his father-in-law, Walter H. Annenberg, former owner of *T.V. Guide* and a former U.S. Ambassador to Great Britain. Far from recoiling in horror, Kabler says, Annenberg's sole and immediate reaction was: "That's a million-dollar idea."

—*Fortune* magazine

AND NOW FOR THE SAP

Latex comes from the Brasiliensis tree, a native of Brazil. It is collected in much the same way as maple syrup, with thin strips of bark cut away, and the 'sap' collected in cups.

Liberia, Malaysia, and Indonesia are the major sources of latex for the U.S., with much of it landing in Baltimore, Maryland.

THE GARDEN STATE?

Perhaps New Jersey should come up with a new motto that proudly proclaims it the Condom Capital, since 90% of all **bags** sold in the U.S. are manufactured there. Trojan Brand Condoms account for over 50% of all condoms sold.

IF THE SAUSAGE FITS

Schmid Laboratories had its start when Julius Schmid bought a troubled sausage-casing business in 1883 and began producing natural skin condoms with the equipment.

DADDY, PICK ME UP

In a gas station rest room the father was cornered when his son asked what the condom machine was.

He answered, "That's a machine that sells containers that fit over a penis."

With the innocence of childhood the boy asked, "How do you get your penis way up there?"

CHOPIN

After reading the instructions on the condom package, the man was a little confused. Since he didn't have an organ he put the **rubber** on his piano.

"It's National Condom Week? I thought it was National Diaphragm Week."

INSIDE A CONDOM FACTORY

Ammonia is the first impression that registers on the brain as you walk through a condom factory. But after you walk past the storage tanks and the myriad of testing stations, what stays with you are the huge dipping machines. A never-ending parade of over 2000 phallic molds called mandrels continuously marches by. These molds are dipped twice into liquid latex and rotated so the latex is evenly spread. When the latex dries, it hardens and each new perfectly formed condom now moves to testing and packaging.

FLIPPING *RUBBERS*

Overheard at Trojan Brand condom plant:

"Money and men. I dream of winning the lottery, and I dream of young men."

—Wilbur Halloway,
grandmother; condom
tester for 16 years

"I'm a Baptist. While I'm doing this I either go over Bible verses in my head, or I think of songs I've heard in church."

—Cindy Gerner,
condom tester for 33 years

EASY MONEY

Remember the days when gas companies actually sent people out to check the cleanliness of service station restrooms? There was the case of a gas station owner who installed a condom vending machine in the ladies' room but never got around to stocking it.

When asked by the inspector to remove it, the owner indignantly replied, "Nothing doing. I get $100 a week from that machine and there has never been a condom in it."

TESTING, ONE TWO THREE, TESTING . . .

Here are all the test condoms must pass before they end up in your wallet—or wherever.

Once the condoms are formed, they are all tested for pinholes by stretching them on stainless steel mandrels and putting them in an electric bath. If a charge passes through, the condom is rejected. Samples are then randomly selected and tested for water leakage, tensile strength, air bursting (wherein they are blown up larger than watermelons) and longevity. Colored condoms are also tested for color fastness.

Lastly, the condoms are submitted to the seal integrity test, which has nothing to do with the honesty of seals, but is used to make sure the foil packages are closed.

Testing is no laughing matter for condom companies. A large percentage of manufacturing costs goes into testing and quality control in order to insure the customer's peace of mind.

ELECTRIC TESTING MACHINE

In 1934, the makers of Trojan Brand Condoms invented a tabletop machine that let customers test condoms.

Once around the **DIAL** becomes a **WATCHWORD**

YOU'VE COME A LONG WAY, BABY

Just as people need to change the way they think, condom packages have changed to keep up with the times.

FOR THAT YUPPIE IN YOUR LIFE

Designer condom cases are available for the man who has everything and doesn't want to give it to anyone.

Filofax Datebook, the pinnacle of Yuppiedom, now includes a space for a condom.

Pet Rubbers—oh, yes! "The first condom that's user-friendly," it comes with a guide on how to teach your pet new tricks.

Safety Shorts—Underwear with a pocket for condoms in case you're ever caught with your pants down.

This hang-tag comes on all safety shorts.

END

APPENDICES #1-4

APPENDIX #1: SYNONYMS

Con-dom/`kən-dəm, `kàṅ-/n: said to have been invented by one Colonel Cundum; a sheath commonly of rubber worn over the penis (as to prevent conception or venereal infection) during coitus.

American Letter
American Tips
Armorial Guise
Armour/Armour Bag
Assurance Caps

Baby Balloons
Bag/Baggie
Balloon
Baudruche
Bishop
Bladder-policies
Buckskin

Cabinet of Love
Calotte d'Assurances
Capote Anglaise
Cheater
Chemisette
Circular Protector
Coat
Cundom
Condrum
Coney Island Whitefish
Cover
Cundum
Cutherean Shield

Dogs
Diving Suit
Dreadnought

Eel-skin
English Hat
English Cloaks
English Overcoats
English Riding Coats
Envelope

Fear-nought
Fish-skin
French Baudruche
French Letter
French Male Safe
French Safe
Frenchy
Frog
Frog Skin

Gant des Dames
Garbage Bags
Glove (Old English)
Grecian Caps
Goody Bags
Gossy
Gun

Hats
Hefty Garbage Bag

Instruments of Safety
Italian Letter

Jo-bag
Johnnie
Joy Bag

Kinga (Swahili)

Latex
Letter
Luble

Machine
Male Pessary
Male Safe
Malthus Caps
Manhole Cover
Meat Casings

Neurodh (Hindi)
Never-failing Engine
Night Caps

One-fingered Glove
One-piece Overcoat

Penis
Peau Divine
Penis Wrapper
Phallic
Port Said Garter
Postocalyptrons
Potent Ally

Preserve
Pro
Propho
Prophylactic
Protectives
Protector

Raincoat
Receptacle for Wild Oats
Redingote Anglaise
Rubber
Rubber Balloon
Rubber Duckie

Safe
Safety
Safety Caps
Safety Sheath
Scumbag
Sheath
Shield
Shoe
Shower-cap
Skin
Spanish Letter
Speciallies
Sweaters

Thimble
Thing
Trousers

Very Tight Trousers

APPENDIX #2: SAFE SEX PRACTICES

Definition of safe sex: Sexual activities that are presumed to be safe are those that do not involve exposing a mucous membrane (rectum, vagina, mouth) to body fluids (blood, semen, vaginal secretions, urine, feces).

Low Risk Behavior:

- Abstinence
- Monogamous relationship with uninfected partner
- Touching, hugging, massage
- Masturbation—alone or with a partner
- Dry kissing—unless there are sores present

Probably Safe Behavior (though only abstinence is 100% safe):

- Vaginal or anal intercourse with a properly used condom
- French kissing (wet), unless sores are present or the kiss is hard enough to draw blood
- Oral sex with a condom or dental dam

High Risk/Unsafe Sexual Behavior

- Vaginal intercourse without a properly used condom with a partner whose drug and sexual history is unknown (or who received blood prior to 1985 when HIV-antibody testing started).
- Oral sex when sores are present around the mouth or on genitals or when there is an exchange of body fluids.
- Rimming, fisting, "water sports"

Note:

1. Alcohol and drugs can impair your judgment and result in practicing unsafe sex. One study shows alcohol might make one more susceptible to the AIDS virus.
2. Anal intercourse is dangerous because it often tears tissue and causes bleeding.
3. The more sex partners and the less you know about their personal history, the higher the risk.
4. Natural lambskin condoms may have a different permeability than latex and may not lend themselves to the same degree of uniformity in manufacture as synthetic materials such as latex. In the interest of prudence, therefore, the FDA requests that natural lambskin condoms not be labeled "for protection against STDs." In other words, they are only marketed as birth control devices.

APPENDIX #3: THE MOST COMMON SEXUALLY TRANSMITTED DISEASES

	CHLAMYDIA	GONORRHEA	GENITAL WARTS	HERPES	SYPHILIS	AIDS
No. new cases yearly	4.6 million	1.8 million	1 million	500,000	90,000	16,000
Symptoms in women	Vaginal discharge, abdominal discomfort, pain during urination.**	Discomfort when urinating, vaginal discharge, abnormal menses.**	Small, painless growths on genitals and anus which may clump together. May also occur inside the vagina without external symptoms.*	Painful blisters on the genitals during the first outbreak, sometimes with fever and aching muscles. Women with sores on the cervix may be unaware of outbreaks.*	In the first stage, reddish-brown sores on the mouth and/or genitals which may disappear, though the bacteria remain; in the second, more infectious stage, a widespread skin rash.*	Extreme fatigue, fever, swollen lymph nodes, weight loss, diarrhea, night sweats, susceptibility to other diseases.*
Symptoms in men	Pain during urination, discharge from penis.*	Discharge from penis, pain during urination.*	Painless growths that usually appear on penis but may also appear on urethra or in rectal area.*	Blisters anywhere on the genitalia, usually on the penis.*	Same as for women.*	Same as for women.*
When symptoms appear	1 to 2 weeks after infection.	2 to 10 days after infection.	3 months to 1 year after infection.	2 weeks to several years after contact.	2 to 6 weeks after infection.	6 months to 8 years after infection.
Diagnosis	Cervical smear; results available within hours.	Culture of secretions from cervix, throat or rectum (depending on the type of intercourse); results available within 2 days.	Visual exam for external warts; Pap test for internal.	Visual examination and/or viral culture.	Blood test.	A blood test can detect antibodies indicating virus presence; it isn't yet known what percentage of carriers develop the disease.
Treatment	10 to 14 days of tetracycline or erythromycin.	Penicillin, although some new strains are resistant to penicillin and must be treated with other antibiotics.	Removal of warts with caustic solution (several treatments may be necessary); electrosurgery or surgery.	No known cure, but can be controlled with the antiviral drug, acyclovir. Women with herpes should have a Pap test every 6 months.	Penicillin or other appropriate antibiotic.	An experimental drug called AZT, which inhibits the growth of the AIDS virus and has been shown to extend life.

APPENDIX #4: HEALTH HOTLINE

NATIONAL PHONE NUMBERS

National Venereal Disease Hotline: 1-800-227-8922
Calif.: 1-800-982-5883
National AIDS Information Hotline: 1-800-342-AIDS (2437)
National Gay Task Force AIDS Inf.: 1-800-221-7044
212-529-1604

National AIDS Network
2033 M Street, N.W.
Washington, D.C. 20036
202-293-2437

National Association
of People With AIDS
2025 I Street, N.W.
Washington, D.C. 20006
202-429-2856

American Red Cross
AIDS Education Office
1730 D Street, N.W.
Washington, D.C. 20006
202-737-8300

Planned Parenthood Federation
of America
810 Seventh Avenue
New York, N.Y. 10019
212-541-7800

Most states and major cities have AIDS information and support groups and local chapters of the Planned Parenthood Associations. For handy reference here are some addresses and phone numbers in major metropolitan areas:

Los Angeles AIDS Project
3670 Wilshire Blvd., Suite 300
L.A., Ca. 90010
213-380-2000

Gay Men's Health Crisis
129 W. 20th Street
New York, N.Y. 10011
212-807-6655

Hispanic AIDS Forum
140 W. 22nd Street, Room 301
New York, N.Y. 10011
212-463-8264

Planned Parenthood Federation:
New York: 212-777-2002
San Francisco: 415-441-5454
Boston: 617-799-5307
Dallas: 214-363-2004

San Francisco AIDS Foundation
333 Valencia Street, 4th Floor
San Francisco, Ca. 94103
415-863-2437

Minority Task Force on AIDS
92 St. Nicholas Avenue Apt. 1B
New York, N.Y. 10026
212-749-2816

Los Angeles: 213-223-4462
Chicago: 312-781-9550
Atlanta: 404-688-9300
Houston: 713-522-3976

ABOUT THE AUTHORS

 usan Zimet and Victor Goodman are escapees from the confines of the corporate advertising world who have formed CIVAN, INC. a company dedicated to the development, marketing and promotion of new ideas and products.

AUTHORS:

Susan Zimet—grew up on Long Island, graduated from State University of New York at Buffalo, worked on Madison Avenue, taught in the Communications Department at State University of New York at New Paltz. Presently lives upstate with her husband, Steve, and their son, Andrew Eli.

Victor Goodman—grew up in the wilds of the Bronx, graduated Bernard Baruch College, toiled for advertising agencies in the U.S., Far East and Africa, and just plain traveled a bit.

ILLUSTRATOR:

Stephanie Silber—grew up on Long Island, studied fine arts and has always enjoyed painting. Worked in various capacities in film, video and theatre. Recently has worked mostly as a researcher and writer and is currently working on her first novel.

For extra copies of this book, please send $5.95 plus $1.00 per book for shipping. This book is available in bulk discount for educational use by libraries, nonprofit and other organizations, and schools. For more information, please contact:
Civan, Inc.
P.O. Box 358,
New Paltz, NY 12561